HOME
HYDROPONICS

© 2021 Quarto Publishing Group USA Inc.
Text © 2021 Tyler Baras

First Published in 2021 by Cool Springs Press, an imprint of The Quarto Group,
100 Cummings Center, Suite 265-D, Beverly, MA 01915, USA.
T (978) 282-9590 F (978) 283-2742 QuartoKnows.com

Cool Springs Press titles are also available at discount for retail, wholesale, promotional, and bulk purchase. For details, contact the Special Sales Manager by email at specialsales@quarto.com or by mail at The Quarto Group, Attn: Special Sales Manager, 100 Cummings Center, Suite 265-D, Beverly, MA 01915, USA.

25 24 23 22 21   1 2 3 4 5

ISBN: 978-0-7603-7038-4

Digital edition published in 2021
eISBN: 978-0-7603-37039-1

Library of Congress Cataloging-in-Publication Data available.

Design: John Hall Design Group, Beverly, MA
Cover Image: Colleen Eversman of 2nd Truth Photography
Photography: Colleen Eversman of 2nd Truth Photography; except page 21, Shutterstock.com

Printed in China

For the **Kitchen, Dining Room, Living Room, Bedroom,** and **Bath**

HOME
HYDROPONICS

SMALL-SPACE DIY GROWING SYSTEMS

TYLER BARAS
Best-selling author of
DIY Hydroponic Gardens

COOL
SPRINGS
PRESS

CONTENTS

INTRODUCTION

MOST HYDROPONIC GARDENS are large contraptions with a maze of PVC pipes and lots of shiny plastic surfaces. My previous book, *DIY Hydroponic Gardens*, includes many designs that fit that description well. These traditional hydroponic garden designs prioritize functionality over aesthetics. In this book I approach the design process with the goal of creating functional artwork, sacrificing neither functionality nor aesthetics of a hydroponic garden.

After living in a very small recreational vehicle (RV) for many years, I grew to despise clutter and began to prioritize owning items that serve many purposes. A home hydroponic garden should not be "clutter" that solely grows plants: a home hydroponic garden should look great, smell great, grow plants and be a unique expression of you and your life! Some of the gardens in this book are made from vintage whiskey boxes and redwood planks salvaged from a 150-year-old grain silo on a farm near my home. There are so many ways to incorporate unique items into a garden design to create a functional piece of artwork with a story you'll love to share.

In the first section of this book, I introduce you to the many benefits of gardening hydroponically and fill you in on the maintenance requirements and location needs of your garden. From there, we'll take a look at the light, climate, and nutritional fundamentals for home hydroponic growing as well as how to select the best plants to grow. In section 3 you'll find step-by-step instructions for building 15 attractive and functional hydroponic gardens for every area of your home, from the living room and kitchen to the bar and bathroom. Section 4 then shares all the practical details of growing effectively and efficiently. You'll get the low-down on system operation components, including how to start your plants, fertilize, clean your system, and troubleshoot issues should any arise. Throughout this book,

you'll also find URLs to pages on my website where you'll be able to find more information about various aspects of hydroponic growing. *Home Hydroponics* has everything you need to build aesthetically pleasing hydroponic gardens to help feed you and your family year-round.

If feel inspired to share your projects, please send me photos of your completed home hydroponic garden. Gardening can sometimes feel like a solitary activity but sharing your garden, building a group of fellow plant enthusiasts and learning from others can allow you to get so much more enjoyment out of gardening!

FARMER TYLER

CONNECT WITH FARMER TYLER:

www.FarmerTyler.com
www.youtube.com/TheFarmerTyler
www.facebook.com/TheFarmerTyler
www.instagram.com/TheFarmerTyler
www.twitter.com/TheFarmerTyler

CONSIDERATIONS FOR SELECTING A GARDEN DESIGN

HYDROPONIC OR TRADITIONAL GARDEN?

I'LL START WITH THIS: no matter how excited you are to learn how to grow hydro-ponically, a hydroponic garden may not always be the best option. A traditional, soil-based garden has many benefits and may be better suited for your indoor garden. It is important to consider the pros and cons of both methods. Many of the systems in this book can be modified to use a soil-based potting mix and operate like a traditional garden. A note on the feasibility of a soil option is provided with each of the building plans found in section 3. Let's look at some of the factors you should consider before diving into building your first hydroponic garden.

AESTHETICS

If a garden is going to be placed in a very visible location it should be subjected to the same stylistic scrutiny that would be applied to any piece of furniture or appliance in a home. I generally think of hydroponic gardens as having a modern, clean look while traditional gardens have a classic, comforting feel. These traits obviously depend on the specific design and personal opinion, but it is important to think if the indoor space already has a decorative theme that would mesh well with a hydroponic or traditional garden.

COST

The startup and maintenance costs of most hydroponic systems are higher than a similarly sized traditional garden. There are some hydro-ponic system designs that are inexpensive, several of which are highlighted in section 3, but the advanced hydroponic garden designs with powerful grow lights and pumps are generally more expensive to build and operate.

FORM FACTOR

It is possible to get very creative with the designs of both hydroponic and traditional gardens. Wall gardens, cascading channels of plants, Ferris wheels . . . there are so many ways to grow a plant, but some system form factors favor either a hydroponic or traditional soil-based garden. A tower garden (see the Bar Tower or Lettuce Locker gardens in section 3 on pages 66 and 140) can be hydroponic or soil-based, but system operation is significantly easier and cleaner using a hydroponic design.

Crop yield from a small corner-shelf hydroponic garden is shown 25 days after transplanting seedlings.

CROP OPTIONS

A hydroponic garden can be designed to grow any plant but that doesn't mean it should be. To take full advantage of a hydroponic system it is best to select crops that excel in hydroponics. The "Crop Selection Charts" in the appendix on page 177 provide recommended crop types and specific varieties that grow well in a hydroponic garden.

YIELD

Hydroponics has the potential to create growing conditions that maximize the yield of a crop. It's possible to do this with a traditional garden as well, but I've personally struggled to match the crop performance I see in hydroponics. Keeping fertility, pH, root temperature, moisture levels, and root zone oxygen levels within an optimal range are much easier in a hydroponic garden.

DIFFICULTY

A common misconception about hydroponics is that it is more difficult than traditional gardening. Some hydroponic garden designs are indeed difficult to manage but other designs, such as the Stream of Greens garden in section 3 on page 54, simply involve filling up the reservoir with water, mixing in some fertilizer, adding some seeds, and then returning two to four weeks later to harvest. Cleaning and restarting the garden can also be much easier! Hydroponic gardens that are designed to be easy can be far easier than any traditional soil-based garden.

CLEANLINESS

This won't come as a surprise, but soil can be messy. Hydroponics is not completely clean either, but I think hydroponics generally comes out ahead in the cleanliness category. Soil-based gardens are often messier to build, maintain, and clean. There are many reasons to clean a garden such as bugs, bad smells or simply wanting new plants, but the process in a traditional garden usually involves removing soil and starting over. In a hydroponic garden it is often possible to replace the nutrient water or replace individual plants without resetting the full garden and making a big mess.

INDOOR GARDEN LOCATIONS

Selecting the appropriate location for a hydroponic indoor garden is critical to its success. Access to light, water, appropriate temperatures, and ease of access are all important considerations.

WINDOWS AND NATURAL LIGHT

All plants need light but not all indoor hydroponic gardens require electricity to provide that light. Placing a garden by a window is a great way to simplify an indoor garden by potentially eliminating the need for a grow light. Unfortunately, not all windows are well suited. In the northern hemisphere the preferred windows for a garden face east, west, or south. In the southern hemisphere the preferred windows for a garden face east, west, or north. A window may only have direct or shaded light for a couple hours per day, which is insufficient for robust plant growth but may be sufficient if the window garden is only used to keep store-bought living herbs alive or grow plants with very low light requirements such as microgreens. See Light in section 2 on page 17 to learn how to measure light levels and see the Crop Selection Charts in the appendix on page 177 for target light levels for popular hydroponic crops.

The other important consideration with window gardens is temperature. The area around a window can get much hotter or colder than other areas in a home. Poorly insulated windows can get very cold in the winter and may create a damaging environment for herbs that prefer warm environments. Periods of intense heat can also be very stressful on plants in a window garden.

SELF-CONTAINED GARDENS: CABINETS, ARMOIRES, AND CLOSETS

A self-contained location such as a cabinet, armoire, pantry, drawer, or locker is great for minimizing the light pollution of a grow light in a living space, but these closed environments create climate management challenges. Self-contained gardens generally require an exhaust fan and depending on the specific fan used, it may generate a lot of noise. The Lettuce Locker and the Cabinet Farm gardens in section 3 on pages 132 and 140 require nearly constant use of an exhaust fan. This noise to some may be a comforting white noise but to others it may be quite annoying. A little humming noise in a kitchen does not bother me much, but I would not want that persistent humming noise in my bedroom when I'm trying to sleep. The air temperature in a self-contained garden will almost always be warmer than the general indoor air temperature due to the heat generated from grow lights. Even with energy-efficient LED grow lights and a powerful exhaust fan, the temperature will likely still be a little warmer in a self-contained garden. This temperature difference can create a challenge for gardeners with homes in warm climates. High temperatures limit the viable crop options for a hydroponic garden. For gardeners in cold climates, a self-contained garden running slightly warmer than inside temperatures may be beneficial.

DIY OR PREMANUFACTURED?

I am a big fan of growing hydroponically whether it is using a DIY or pre-manufactured hydroponic garden. This book focuses on DIY options but for some gardeners the best option may be a pre-manufactured garden. However, DIY hydroponic gardens are the clear winner when it comes to customization. The ability to repurpose items such as tables, scrap wood, and porcelain bowls into beautiful DIY hydroponic gardens enables a level of customization and personalization that a pre-manufactured garden cannot match.

FUNCTIONAL SURFACES: TABLETOPS, COUNTERS, AND DESKS

Under the category of functional surfaces I include tabletops, kitchen counters, and desk surfaces. These surfaces are used for food preparation, eating, working, or some task that requires the space be versatile. Placing a large garden on a functional surface can significantly reduce the versatility of that surface. This tradeoff should not be ignored when selecting a location for an indoor garden. The Stream of Greens garden in section 3 on page 54 takes up a significant amount of kitchen counter space but it is capable of yielding several salads per week. In general, I prefer that gardens designed for these functional surfaces be mobile or can be used as a functional surface themselves. For example, the Dinner Table garden in section 3 on page 76 has a large flat-top surface that can be used to hold condiments, drinks, or dinner table decorations.

BELOW TABLES

Placing a garden below a functional surface is a great way to preserve that surface space while taking advantage of the underutilized space below. One of my favorite places for a "below table" garden is an end table in a living room. The open space under an end table is often used to store television remotes and books, both of which can be easily stored in another location to frees up that space for a garden. Finding another spot for a television remote is a small tradeoff but there are bigger tradeoffs to consider when placing a garden under a dining table or coffee table. The benefit of open space under a coffee table may not seem immediately evident but after kicking the base of a garden under a table enough times, you'll start to remember why many tables have open space underneath. The Lift Top Coffee Table described in section 3 on page 108 is one of my favorite gardens, and the tradeoff of reduced under-table space in exchange for a coffee table garden is well worth it to me. But I think it is very important gardeners know the tradeoffs involved before building a garden under a table.

BATHROOMS

A bathroom is one of the best locations for a hydroponic garden. Bathrooms already have convenient sources of water and drains to flush out spent nutrient solution. The periods of high humidity when someone takes a hot shower or bath are generally harmless to the garden, if not beneficial at times, and most bathrooms are well ventilated to remove humidity. Bathrooms are also frequently trafficked, which means the garden will likely get a lot of attention and care. The only downside of a garden in a bathroom is the potential food safety concerns of growing edible produce in a bathroom. The Bathroom Flower Garden shown in the section 3 build guides on page 150 is used to grow flowers and scented herbs, neither of which are intended for consumption. For homeowners with a spare

bathroom that is not used for typical bathroom purposes, that space could be devoted to food production and the entire space including sink, toilet, and bathtub could be converted into hydroponic gardens!

WALLS

One of the biggest challenges with wall gardens is their weight. A very heavy wall garden may not be safe to mount on a wall or will require heavy-duty wood screws positioned on wall studs. Water is heavy, over 8 pounds per gallon, so it is important to mount the garden on studs and not rely on drywall mounts. The depth of a wall garden, or how far out it protrudes from a wall, can also be an issue depending on the specific mounting location. The Picture Frame wall garden in section 3 on page 82 is placed in a dining room so it needed to be shallow enough not to get in the way of people accessing the dinner table. Similar issues arise when positioning a wall garden in a hallway. Positioning a wall garden above a couch is a great option as long as it is high enough to avoid risks of someone hitting their head on the garden. Another challenge with wall gardens is power supply. It can look unsightly to see a long power cord dangling on a wall supplying power to a garden. The use of power cord raceways can greatly improve the aesthetics of a wall garden.

CORNER SHELF

Corner shelves are great since they are typically used to display art or books and the conversion of some of the shelf space into a garden does not come with a major tradeoff. Corner shelves are also nice for a garden because the grow light can be directed toward the corner to minimize the amount of light escaping into the living space. Choosing a corner near a window can reduce the need for a grow light but including a grow light will expand the crop options.

CEILING MOUNTED

A ceiling-mounted garden is challenging to install but can make use of underutilized space. A ceiling mounted grow light with hanging pots below can provide light for the plants and act as the primary light source for a room. Accessing the hanging garden can be a challenge, but if it's creatively designed it could include pots with visible water-level indicators to make it easy to know when a specific hanging pot needs attention.

CLOSET

Closet gardens face some of the same challenges as mentioned with cabinets and self-contained gardens. The heat generation of grow lights in a closed space makes it difficult to grow crops without the addition of exhaust fans or, in extreme cases, air-conditioning units. The focus of this book is gardens that are positioned in visible locations that need to be both beautiful and functional, so a tucked away closet garden is a little out of scope, but they are definitely a viable option for growing produce indoors.

CONSIDERATIONS

The Stream of Greens garden in section 3 on page 54 is one of the most productive hydroponic garden designs shown in this book. This garden has a 5¼-square-foot footprint, large enough to provide multiple salads each week, but allocating this much space to an indoor garden may not be practical in small homes.

YIELD POTENTIAL

Depending on crop selection, system selection, light levels, climate, and system maintenance, a hydroponic garden can yield anywhere between 1 to 23 pounds of salad greens per square foot per year (5½ to 110 kg/m2/year). Most home hydroponic gardens can expect yields around 3¾ to 6 pounds of salad greens per square foot per year (18 to 27.5 kg/m2/year). I eat at least ½ pound (0.23 kg) of salad per week, meaning I need 1¼ square feet of a superoptimized garden to meet my salad needs, and if I'm considering a typical yield of a home hydroponic garden, I'd need 4½ to 7½ square feet. The story is very different when I think about my weekly herb consumption. I rarely eat more than a few ounces (85 grams) of herbs per week, and this is much easier to achieve with a home hydroponic garden.

CROP FLEXIBILITY

The primary factors restricting crop options in a hydroponic garden are vertical growing space and light levels. Some hydroponic garden designs, especially vertical towers, may struggle to support the weight of a crop's canopy or may have limited space for root growth, making it difficult to grow long-term crops with extensive root systems. I typically see new gardeners select a garden design before deciding which crops to grow, but if there is a specific desired crop it is important to select a design capable of meeting that crop's needs.

MAINTENANCE REQUIRED

Most of the soil-based gardens I've managed throughout the years require watering once per week or at least once every two weeks. Most hydroponic gardens require a similar amount of maintenance, but depending on design choices, the range of time between garden maintenance can be a couple days to a couple months! The two biggest factors affecting the amount of maintenance required for a hydroponic garden are a specific crop's growth cycle and the planting density relative to reservoir size.

A hydroponic garden that packs in a lot of plants in a relatively small reservoir will quickly deplete the nutrient solution, requiring frequent water and fertilizer additions. As the crops mature their fertilizer and water needs increase, which can increase the maintenance frequency. Crops that grow quickly such as microgreens can go from seed to harvest in as little as six days, requiring the gardener to clean and seed the garden every week to keep the harvest.

SYSTEM STABILITY/ROBUSTNESS

For system stability I consider the following questions:

- → How long can the system keep plants alive if there is a power outage?
- → Are there a lot of moving parts that could potentially fail?
- → Does the system have an irrigation system with small emitters that could potentially clog?

If the garden is selected purely for system stability then the selection often narrows down to a floating raft or deep-water culture system since they can operate without power, have no moving parts, and have no small emitters. Most of the eye-catching mad-scientist systems that have moving conveyors, rotating Ferris wheels, or high-pressure misting systems are a lot of fun but are not very stable. For me, the primary purpose of a home hydroponic garden is aesthetics and then functionality, so I'm okay with building a complex garden that may need frequent attention in exchange for it being amazing and eye-catching. If your primary purpose is to grow plants while not being an eyesore, then a simple system design such as a floating raft garden may be the best option.

AESTHETICS

Large plastic boxes and exposed PVC pipes are common in most hydroponic gardens, but it can be difficult to use these elements to build a hydroponic garden that is beautiful enough to place in a living space. These clunky plastic hydroponic gardens are great for garages and yards, but for hydroponic gardens placed in a living space I prefer to hide the plastic components with wood, metal, and glass/acrylic. Aesthetics is obviously a personal opinion and the build guides in this book leave space for individuals to tweak the design in a way that suits their space best.

An image is great for communicating the physical beauty of a garden but unfortunately an image cannot capture the sounds generated by a garden. A home hydroponic garden can add to the soundscape of a living space with gentle trickling water sounds or it can pollute a living space with noise. The humming sounds of water pumps, air pumps, circulation fans, and exhaust fans can be a nuisance depending on the location of a system and, of course, the overall volume of the humming noises. The build guides in section 3 on page 33 include notes on the sound generated by each garden to help you select a garden that adds both physical and auditory beauty to your home!

INDOOR GROWING FUNDAMENTALS

WHEN GROWING OUTDOORS my strategy for success is testing many crops and varieties to find out what grows well in my local conditions during a specific season. In an outdoor garden there are usually limited options for modifying the light levels and climate so finding what grows well in the existing conditions is usually the best option. Variety selection is also important for an indoor garden, but indoors there are many other ways to control the success of a garden. To properly make use of this increased control it is important for an indoor gardener to understand the indoor growing fundamentals including light, climate, and nutrients.

LIGHT

PHOTOPERIOD, INTENSITY, AND SPECTRUM

The three fundamentals of light in horticulture are photoperiod (duration), intensity (quantity), and spectrum (quality). The interaction between these three fundamentals can have drastic effects on crop growth.

Photoperiod: The photoperiod is the amount of time a plant receives light each day. Photoperiod is one of the ways plants sense the changing of seasons in nature. Depending on the crop, a shift in photoperiod may signal it to delay flowering or possibly trigger it to start flowering earlier. Some plants do not have a strong response to photoperiod; these plants are classified as day neutral or photoperiod insensitive. See the Crop Selection Charts in the appendix on page 177 to find recommended photoperiods for popular hydroponic crops. Besides inducing or inhibiting reproduction (flowering), photoperiod has a direct influence on the total amount of light a plant receives throughout a day.

Intensity: Light intensity, or light quantity, is either measured by the instantaneous intensity (light per second) or the total light received over a day. For example, a garden hose releasing 1 gallon per second (instantaneous flow) that is left on for 6 hours in a day emits a daily total of 21,600 gallons (1 gal/s x 60 s/min x 60 min/hr x 6 hr). For light, the instantaneous measurement is called the photosynthetic photon flux density (PPFD), which uses the unit micromole per square meter per second (umol/m2/s). The cumulative measurement is called the daily light integral (DLI), which uses the unit mole per square meter per day (mol/m2/d). All plants have preferred ranges for PPFD and DLI. A specific DLI can be achieved in many ways depending on PPFD and photoperiod. Following are three examples of ways to reach a DLI of 12 mol/m2/d:

➡ PPFD of 417 umol/m2/s and photoperiod of 8 hours

➡ PPFD of 278 umol/m2/s and photoperiod of 12 hours

➡ PPFD of 209 umol/m2/s and photoperiod of 16 hours

A photoperiod-sensitive crop may have fewer options for reaching its target DLI. For example, cilantro grows well indoors at a DLI between 12 to 17 mol/m2/d, but the longer the photoperiod, the earlier cilantro begins to flower. Cilantro flowers are edible and taste great, but most gardeners grow cilantro for the leaves. A photoperiod around 8 hours can enable a cilantro plant to grow leaves without flowering for over 2 months but reaching the target DLI in only 8 hours requires a high PPFD, which means purchasing a powerful grow light. Alternatively the grower can accept that their cilantro may flower within two months and use a less powerful light on a 16-hour photoperiod. Cilantro also tends to flower earlier in warm conditions. If an indoor garden is not properly ventilated and the more powerful grow light creates a significantly warmer environment, the cilantro may still be triggered to flower early.

One of the key details in measuring light intensity for plants is the focus on photosynthetic photons. PPFD and DLI only measure the total amount of light delivered to a plant in a specific range of wavelengths capable of powering photosynthesis in a plant.

Spectrum: Spectrum, or light quality, is one of the most fun topics to explore in indoor gardening. A light might appear to the human eye as a single color but it often consists of many wavelengths of light. Specific wavelength ranges can trigger unique responses in plants and with the proper equipment, a grower can adjust the spectrum, or mix of wavelengths contributing to that light, to get targeted reactions in a plant. Changes in spectrum can alter a plant's flavor, leaf texture, leaf color, leaf size, plant height, and other growth traits. Adjusting light spectrum to steer plant growth is an advanced topic and only covered briefly in this book. For a home garden I prioritize selecting a grow light with an aesthetically pleasing spectrum that can also grow a wide range of plants.

FARMER TYLER

Learn more about horticultural lighting in Farmer Tyler's video series Plants & Light. Visit http://farmer-tyler.com/plants-light

MEASURING LIGHT

Measuring light levels in an indoor garden can help a gardener select crops well suited to those light levels or potentially modifying the garden (adding/removing more grow lights) to achieve light levels suitable for a desired crop. One of the most common mistakes made by new indoor gardeners is providing insufficient light. Most grow lights come with technical specification sheets that provide information on their output and the appropriate distancing of the grow light to the plant canopy. This information is usually sufficient for starting a new indoor garden but for troubleshooting purposes and satiating curiosity, it is nice to have a light meter. A light meter can remove all of the guesswork involved in determining if your indoor garden has sufficient light. Light meters typically measure light either in lux or PPFD.

LUX AND FOOTCANDLES

Lux (metric) and footcandles (imperial) are the most common units for measuring light in nonhorticultural applications. These units measure light based on how the human eye perceives it. The human eye is most sensitive to green light. Lux and footcandles are great for determining if there is enough light in a space where humans work or live, but these units can be misleading when determining light levels for plants since green light is not especially efficient at powering photosynthesis.

PHOTOSYNTHETIC PHOTON FLUX DENSITY (PPFD)

The photosynthetic photon flux density (PPFD) measures the amount of light per square meter, similar to lux, but the wavelengths of light are not weighted by the way the human eye perceives light but rather, what wavelengths are capable of powering photosynthesis. PPFD is a more useful unit for measuring light intensity when working with plants.

Some light measuring applications enable smartphones to measure lux. Use the Conversion Tables in the appendix on page 176 to convert this measurement to PPFD. The "Crop Selection Charts" in the appendix on page 177 provide recommended PPFD values for popular hydroponic crops.

LIGHT METER OPTIONS

Most beginning indoor gardeners opt to invest in a lux meter since they are much less expensive and, in general, they can do the job of indicating if a garden is receiving sufficient light. As mentioned, lux is a measurement of how the human eye perceives light and not a measurement of the amount of light is being output that is relevant to plant growth. To make the best use of a lux measurement I recommend using the Conversion Tables in the appendix on page 176 to convert the lux measurement into an approximate PPFD.

The preferred light meter for grow lights is a PAR meter. PAR stands for photosynthetically active radiation; this is the range of wavelengths capable of powering photosynthesis. A PAR meter can easily be ten times more expensive than a typical lux meter and may be overkill for the light measuring needs of a home hydroponic gardener.

TARGET LIGHT LEVELS

The daily light integral (DLI) is the primary unit used when discussing target light levels for a crop as it considers both the instantaneous intensity of the light (PPFD) and how long the crop is exposed to that light (photoperiod). The DLI can be measured directly with a DLI meter that records light levels over a 24-hour period or the DLI can be calculated using instantaneous light intensity (PPFD or lux) and photoperiod. The following example starts with a lux measurement, but if you have a PAR meter capable of measuring PPFD, please skip to step 2.

1 Convert lux to PPFD. Conversion factors for specific light sources can be found in the Conversion Tables in the appendix on page 176. For this example, let's assume we measure a lux of 10,000 from sunlight next to a window. The conversion factor for sunlight is 0.019, so 10,000 x 0.019 = 190 umol/m2/s.

2 Measure the amount of time the garden receives that amount of light. With a grow light it is easy since the light can be programmed for a specific on-time, but with sunlight it is necessary to visually monitor how long the garden receives light. The intensity of sunlight will change throughout the day in a specific location making it more complicated (but possible) to calculate the DLI. But for simplicity let's assume a window location receives five hours of 190 umol/m2/s.

3 Multiply the PPFD value by the amount of time (in seconds) to get umol/m2/day.

> → 5 hours = 18,000 seconds (60 seconds x 60 minutes x 5 hours)

> → 190 umol/m2/s x 18,000 seconds = 3,420,000 umol/m2/d

4 Divide the total umol/m2/d by 1,000,000 to convert value to mol/m2/d.

> → 3,420,000 / 1,000,000 = 3.42 mol/m2/d

5 Compare the calculated DLI (mol/m2/d) value to recommended DLI values for popular hydroponic crops available in the Crop Selection Charts in the appendix on page 177.

The target DLI for a crop should be achieved using a photoperiod and instantaneous light intensity (PPFD) that are appropriate for that crop. The target DLI range for popular hydroponic crops can be found in the Crop Selection Charts in the appendix on page 177 along with appropriate ranges for PPFD and photoperiod to achieve that DLI. If you're unable to find a target DLI for a specific crop, I recommend using the following table with general DLI targets by crop group. There are some crops within each of these groups that have needs outside of the target range but, in general, these target ranges are appropriate for the majority of crops within the group.

CROP GROUP	TARGET DLI RANGE
Microgreens	6–12 mol/m²/day
Leafy Greens	12–30 (generally 17–25) mol/m²/day
Flowering Crops	17–45 (generally 25–35) mol/m²/day

GROW LIGHTS

The Kelvin color temperature scale is not the best way to judge a light for growing plants, but it is very helpful when selecting a light for a living space. Warm colors on the lower end of the spectrum are often described as cozy and comfortable while cooler colors on the high end of the spectrum may be described as bright and energizing.

Many of the standard lighting options for interior spaces are capable of growing plants but using a light not designed for growing plants can be challenging. A grow light is often designed for wet or at least humid environments. A traditional light may not last long in humid conditions or, in the worst case, it could create a serious safety issue.

	KELVIN COLOR TEMPERATURE	HEAT GENERATION	INTENSITY	NOTES
PRESSURE SODIUM (HPS)	2000–2200	High	High	Great for commercial horticulture but less appropriate for home hydroponic gardens.
CERAMIC METAL HALIDE (CMH)	3200–5500	High	Medium–High	Great for commercial horticulture and home grow tents that permit positioning the grow light at least 1 foot above max crop height. CMH generates a broad well-balanced spectrum ideal for a wide range of crops.
COOL WHITE FLUORESCENT	3000–4500	Medium	Low–Medium	The use of fluorescent grow lights is increasingly less common as most growers make the switch to LED grow lights. There are many fluorescent bulb options; the most popular horticultural bulb is the T5 HO (high output). Fluorescent lights generate a broad well-balanced spectrum.
WARM WHITE FLUORESCENT	2000–3000			
DAYLIGHT LED	4500–6000	Low–High	Low–High	LED grow lights have taken over the horticultural lighting industry over the past decade. LED grow lights can achieve high light intensities while generating minimal heat, making them great for home hydroponic gardens with limited space between the light and the crop.
BRIGHT WHITE LED	3000–4500			
WARM WHITE LED	2000–3000			

CLIMATE

Although there is less variation in climate indoors than there is outdoors, there is still some variation in each individual home based on geographic locations, seasons, and climate control equipment. Most of the home hydroponic gardens described in this book do not have the ability to modify the growing climate and the plants are subject to the general temperature and humidity already present in the living space. I recommend selecting crops that grow well in a home's existing climate instead of trying to modify the climate to suit a specific crop.

AIR TEMPERATURE

The optimal air temperature varies greatly from crop to crop but, most popular hydroponic crops can tolerate the air temperatures commonly observed in a home. Warm temperatures can accelerate growth to an extent but in very warm conditions there may be issues with excessive stem or leaf elongation and premature bolting (flowering). Cooler temperatures typically slow growth and, in extreme conditions, can damage or even kill a crop.

Measuring Air Temperature: Position the thermometer near or within the crop canopy to accurately measure the air temperature that the crop is experiencing. Small Bluetooth thermometers are one of my favorite garden gadgets as they can easily be positioned in the crop canopy and they relay measurements to your smartphone or remote monitor for easy viewing.

Target Levels: 65–80 degrees F

WATER TEMPERATURE

Regulating the water temperature in a hydroponic garden is one of the best tools in a hydroponic grower's toolbelt, but in practice it is usually very difficult to meaningfully augment the water temperature without expensive equipment. There is a lot of research showing the capacity to grow healthy crops in suboptimal air temperatures as long as a plant's root temperature is maintained within a target range. For the home hydroponic grower, the only easily accessible option for augmenting water temperature is adding a simple aquarium water heater. Unfortunately, the water temperature concerns are rarely due to the water being too cold (especially in a home). Warm water temperatures can have a range of detrimental effects including increased pathogen pressure in the root zone, reduced oxygen availability to roots, increased development of biofilms, and several physiological disorders including premature bolting (flowering) and elongated growth.

Measuring Water Temperature: A dedicated thermometer to constantly monitor water temperature is not necessary in a home hydroponic garden. A simple cooking thermometer can be used for spot temperature checks and most pH/EC meters (more on these later) have built-in thermometers.

Target Levels: Optimal range = 65–70 degrees F. Tolerable range = 55–85 degrees F. Over 85 degrees F is possible, but it's very challenging.

HUMIDITY

Humidity can be thought of as the gas pedal for plant growth. Low humidity pushes down the gas pedal while high humidity can slow growth to an idle pace. It may seem like low humidity is best to maximize plant growth but not all plant systems can keep up with the increased growth rate. One of the especially slow processes is the uptake of the plant nutrient calcium, which is used to build cell walls. In low humidity conditions when a plant is trying to grow full speed it may be quickly forming new cells, but the transportation of calcium to build the new cell walls is lagging behind. These new cells, lacking sufficient calcium, fail to hold their shape and burst. This phenomenon can be observed as tip burn in many crops. In high humidity conditions tip burn can also occur as it is difficult for plants to pull up more nutrient solution (the source of calcium) when they're struggling to push out water vapor from their leaves into the humid air.

Measuring Humidity: Measure humidity levels as close to the crop canopy as possible to get measurements that reflect the climate the crop is actually experiencing.

Target Levels: 40%–80%

CARBON DIOXIDE (CO2)

Plants use carbon dioxide in the air to build sugar molecules. These sugar molecules are transported throughout the plant to provide energy for a wide range of processes. In 2019 the average atmospheric carbon dioxide levels were a little over 400 parts per million (ppm), but plants such as tomatoes can be far more productive when grown in conditions with carbon dioxide levels over 1000 ppm. In my home I often measure carbon dioxide levels over 1000 ppm, with the only significant carbon dioxide contributions coming from me and my dogs. Humans exhale a lot of carbon dioxide and simply being around your plants for a few minutes can raise the carbon dioxide levels to nearly 1000 ppm. There are many ways to increase the carbon dioxide levels in an indoor garden besides breathing on your plants though; one of my favorites is adding mushroom production to the garden. Mushrooms, like humans, also release carbon dioxide and pairing a small mushroom farm with a home hydroponic garden is a great way to maintain elevated carbon dioxide levels (see the Cabinet Farm in section 3 on page 132).

Measuring Carbon Dioxide: A home hydroponic gardener does not need to measure carbon dioxide levels to successfully operate their garden.

Target Levels: 400–1500 ppm

AIRFLOW

While a small fan moving air in a garden will not significantly change the temperature and humidity in the room, it can help make the climate in the room more homogenous. As plants transpire they create small pockets of high humidity air around their leaves. These pockets of high humidity air can restrict additional transpiration and slow growth. A small fan can break apart these pockets of humid air.

Measuring Airflow: While there are tools for precisely measuring airflow in an indoor garden, an easier and almost equally effective way of determining if there is adequate airflow is looking for visible leaf movement. A gentle rustling of leaves in the canopy is a sure sign that the home hydroponic garden has sufficient airflow.

Target Levels: 0.1 m/s or visible leaf movement

NUTRIENTS

Although there are examples of growing systems with hydroponic features dating back thousands of years, such as the Aztec hydroponic floating islands of the 10th century, the majority of hydroponic systems popular today were not possible until the early 20th century. In the first two decades of the 20th century there were huge advancements in fertilizer science with the commercialization of the Ostwald and Haber-Bosch process. These processes made it possible to turn the highly abundant nitrogen in Earth's atmosphere into a concentrated nitrogen fertilizer.

Synthetic fertilizers have greatly increased the world's food production, but they are also responsible for a large percentage of human-caused greenhouse gas emissions. There are no doubt tradeoffs with modern agriculture and these tradeoffs extend to the decisions made when managing a home hydroponic garden. The fertilizer management in a hydroponic system can be optimized to eliminate runoff and significantly reduce water usage relative to a traditional garden but to take full advantage of these benefits requires advanced water analysis equipment and a very advanced understanding of fertilizer chemistry. For a home hydroponic garden, the goal is to make the most of your hydroponic fertilizer and minimize the detrimental environmental effects by making smart fertilizer management decisions using practical equipment.

NUTRIENTS TLDR (TOO LONG, DIDN'T READ)

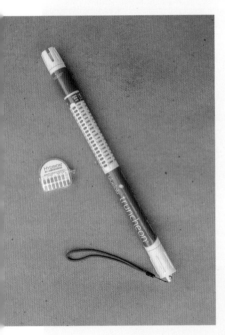

WHAT FERTILIZER?

Ninety-nine percent of home hydroponic gardens will perform well with a basic one-part liquid or dry fertilizer designed specifically for hydroponics. It is very important the fertilizer is made for hydroponics or else it likely will not contain all of the essential nutrients. Organic hydroponics is very challenging and not recommended for new growers.

WHAT EQUIPMENT?

The following equipment is not necessary for most home hydroponic gardens if:

➡ You're using standard hydroponic fertilizer at recommended rates.

➡ You're using a clean, potable water source.

But if you're interested in monitoring the water quality in your hydroponic garden for system troubleshooting, optimizing growth, or simply out of curiosity, I recommend the following equipment for new growers:

➡ EC (electrical conductivity) truncheon: They only turn on when dipped in water and can perform well for years without maintenance.

➡ pH test strips: These are less precise than digital probes but are far less expensive and are sufficient for most home hydroponic gardens.

HOW MUCH?

Follow the instructions on hydroponic fertilizer packaging. The listed rates are often higher than necessary, so I often use one-half to three-fourths the recommended rate and see no difference in growth. If you decide to get equipment to monitor EC and pH, please refer to the Crop Selection Charts in the appendix on page 177 for recommended EC and pH ranges for specific hydroponic crops.

MEASURING FERTILIZER CONCENTRATIONS AND PH

EC

The most common measuring system of fertilizer concentration in a hydroponic system is based on the electrical conductivity (EC) of the nutrient solution. Most of the individual components in a hydroponic fertilizer are classified as salts (yes, like table salt but also no, not like table salt!). A salt is a compound made from a cation (positively charged ion) and an anion (negatively charged ion). For example, table salt is sodium chloride. Sodium is the cation and chloride is the anion. When a salt dissolves in water the cation and anion are pulled apart by water molecules. The addition of salt to water improves the ability of electricity to travel through that water, which is known as electrical conductivity. An EC meter can measure the electrical conductivity of water and provide an indication of how much salt is dissolved in the irrigation water. One additional note to this very simplified lesson on fertilizer salt chemistry is that not all dissolved salts contribute equally to the electrical conductivity of a nutrient solution. This is why the EC is simply an indicator of how much salt is dissolved in the nutrient solution and is not a precise measurement since the EC meter cannot determine the specific salts contributing to the electrical conductivity.

Measuring EC is not essential for managing a hydroponic garden, but the ability to measure EC enables a hydroponic gardener to use alternative nutrient-solution management techniques besides simply flushing out the system and replacing it every couple of weeks. See Fertilizer Maintenance in section 4 on page 164 for more information on nutrient solution management techniques. EC meters can be relatively inexpensive compared to other digital meters used in hydroponic gardening. My favorite EC meter is the truncheon style stick meter that turns on automatically when it's dipped in water. Most of the truncheon style EC meters are strong enough to withstand rough handling and can even be used as a mixing stick when you're stirring in fertilizer additions.

TDS AND PPM

Another popular measuring system for fertilizer concentration in hydroponics is total dissolved solids (TDS). TDS uses the unit parts per million (ppm). TDS meters measure the electrical conductivity of a nutrient solution and then convert that measurement to estimate how many parts of fertilizer are present per million parts of water. As previously mentioned, the EC is simply an indicator of fertilizer concentration, but TDS attempts to provide a specific number for the number of parts of fertilizer that are present. To do this, TDS meter manufacturers pick a standard solution with a known parts per million for specific salts and then use the EC measurement of that standard to estimate the parts per million for all nutrient solutions. This is problematic since not all growers are using the same fertilizer and not all TDS meter manufacturers are using the same conversion rate for EC to ppm. For this reason I generally recommend new growers use EC to avoid the conversion confusion. If you already have a TDS meter and want to use the recommended EC ranges provided in this book

IMPORTANT TERMINOLOGY!

Nutrient Solution: The mix of fertilizer and water at a concentration appropriate for direct use in a hydroponic system.

Stock Solution: A highly concentrated mix of fertilizer and water that's typically 50 to 200 times the recommended concentration used in a nutrient solution.

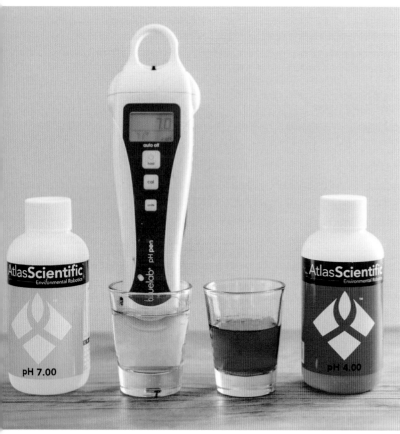

Whether you use an expensive or less expensive pH probe, it is important to buy calibration solutions to check the accuracy and calibrate the probe.

Basil will often show signs of an iron deficiency when grown in a nutrient solution with a pH greater than 6.5.

Measuring pH is not always essential, but one of the first troubleshooting steps for determining the root cause of a nutrient problem is testing pH. The least expensive option for testing pH is to use paper test strips. Paper test strips may not be able to provide a precise pH measurement accurate to several decimal places (e.g., 5.855) but they can provide a general measurement to indicate if the pH is far outside a pH range suitable for healthy crop growth (e.g., below 4 or above 7).

Digital pH meters are often fragile and finicky. They need to be handled gently and frequently calibrated (every two to four weeks) to ensure accuracy. The prices for digital pH probes range greatly, but in my experience the more expensive probes are often less fragile and more stable, requiring less frequent calibrations to maintain accuracy.

A third pH testing option is to use color-changing liquids. I do not recommend this option for hydroponics, however. Color-changing test liquids are typically made for testing clear water samples and hydroponic fertilizers are rarely clear, making it potentially difficult to determine if the results are due to the pH or existing color of the nutrient solution.

use the Conversion Tables in the appendix on page 176. The manual for a TDS/ppm meter typically indicates which EC to ppm conversion scale it uses.

PH

The nutrient solution may contain all of the essential nutrients for plant growth, but a pH that's too high or too low can tie up the nutrients in a variety of ways, making them inaccessible to the plant. For most hydroponic crops a target pH between 5.5 to 6.5 is sufficient. For gardeners using a digital pH meter who are interested in a specific target, most leafy greens and flowering crops grow well at a pH of 5.8. Some crops are more sensitive to pH than others. One of the most common pH-sensitive hydroponic crops is basil.

FERTILIZER SELECTION

There are three big questions when selecting a fertilizer:

Question 1: Do you want an organic or a conventional fertilizer?

I have managed many commercial and home hydroponic systems using certified organic inputs and while it is definitely possible, I would not recommend it for home growers. There are few organic fertilizer products that work well in hydroponic gardens and the ones that do are much more expensive than conventional options. Organic hydroponic gardens sometimes produce superior crops but more often they produce inferior crops that taste bitter as a result of the increased stress they experience during the growing process. Depending on the manufacturing process, organic fertilizers may not even be more environmentally friendly.

Question 2: Do you want liquid or dry fertilizer?

Nearly all of the liquid hydroponic fertilizers (besides organic options) are created by mixing dry fertilizer salts into water. A hydroponic grower can purchase a liquid with salts mixed in or they can purchase the dry salts and mix them as needed.

LIQUID	DRY
More expensive	Less expensive
Ready to use	Requires mixing into water before use
Less concentrated, requires more storage space	More concentrated, requires less storage space
Potentially shorter shelf life	Long shelf life

I recommend new growers start with a dry fertilizer option as it is much less expensive and equally capable of growing great hydroponic crops. The only time I recommend a liquid fertilizer is for school hydroponic gardens as I aim to make the operation of the garden as easy as possible for young students.

Question 3: How much control do you want for adjusting the recipe?

Fertilizers are often described by the number of parts required to create a complete nutrient solution. A one-part fertilizer includes all of the essential nutrients required for plant growth premixed in a single product whether that is a dry powder or liquid concentrate. A two-part fertilizer requires two components to create a nutrient solution with all of the essential nutrients. Increasing the number of parts increases a grower's control of the fertilizer recipe because they can increase or decrease the amount of one part relative to others to increase or decrease the concentration of a specific nutrient within the nutrient solution. Some commercial hydroponic farms use 11 or more different components to create their nutrient solution enabling them to precisely control the concentration of each nutrient, but this degree of control is not necessary for a home hydroponic garden. All of the crops shown in the hydroponic gardens detailed in section 3 on page 33 were grown using a one-part fertilizer. When selecting a one-part fertilizer it may be necessary to choose between one designed for vegetative growth or reproductive/flowering growth. It is definitely possible to grow healthy vegetative crops (such as lettuce) using a flowering recipe, and it is also possible to grow great flowering crops (such as tomatoes) with a vegetative recipe. Select a recipe that is appropriate for the majority of the crop you plan to grow but know that most of the popular hydroponic vegetable crops will grow well using any fertilizer designed for hydroponics.

In the Fertilizer Maintenance in section 4 on page 164, you'll be introduced to the different watering and fertilization strategies noted in each of the DIY projects.

PLANT SELECTION

Picking appropriate plants for your hydroponic garden or picking a hydroponic garden appropriate for the plants you want to grow is essential if you want to make the most out of your hydroponic garden. When selecting a plant for your hydroponic garden the big considerations are plant size, root oxygen demand, life cycle, light requirement, and climate.

PLANT SIZE

Plant size includes both the shoot (aboveground) and root systems of a plant. It is important to consider both the vertical and horizontal space requirements for the shoot. A small hydroponic cabinet will likely not be able to provide the vertical space required for a traditional 6-foot-tall tomato plant, but it may be suitable for a dwarf tomato variety that reaches a maximum height of ten inches. A skinny windowsill garden will likely not provide the horizontal space required for a large 8-inch-diameter butterhead lettuce, but it may be suitable for a dwarf romaine variety that reaches a maximum diameter of 4 inches!

The size of a plant's root system is usually not a concern in hydroponic gardens, but when it is an issue it can lead to permanent damage either to the growing system or your home! Root crops such as radishes, carrots, and beets can be grown in hydroponic systems, but they may quickly find themselves constricted in their container or plug holder. A 1-inch hydroponic seedling cube can start a radish plant, but the diameter of the mature radish will likely exceed one inch. This doesn't seem like a big problem, but one small radish can exert a lot of force as it tries to ex-

pand—enough force to crack a thick plastic plant holder! Some root systems are very aggressive; beyond destroying their plastic container, they can grow so large they block the water flow in a hydroponic garden, potentially blocking water flow to neighboring plants or blocking drainage pipes, perhaps leading to a messy flood. See the Crop Selection Charts in the appendix on page 177 for information on the shoot and root systems of specific hydroponic crops.

ROOT OXYGEN DEMAND

Root oxygen demand is a very important consideration when selecting a plant for a hydroponic garden because different plants can have drastically different root oxygen demands and the root oxygen that's available varies greatly by hydroponic garden design. Some plants are like a betta fish, a popular pet fish that can live in small aquariums without mechanical aeration, but other plants are far less tolerant of low oxygen environments. The Plant Selection Charts in the appendix on page 176 provide information on the root oxygen demand of various hydroponic crops. Generally, the larger the plant, the greater its oxygen demand. The oxygen demand is greatest when a plant is actively taking up water and transpiring during the day. At night the oxygen demand decreases, and, in many cases, it is okay to turn off aeration equipment when plants are not exposed to light.

This hydroponic garden provides plenty of room for root growth, allowing these mint cuttings to grow unrestricted for many months. Limited root space is not a common issue, but when it is an issue, it can create serious problems for both your garden and home.

LIFE CYCLE

The life cycle of a crop affects the maintenance required. To maintain a consistent supply of microgreens, a crop that has a life cycle of a few weeks or less, requires nearly weekly seeding and system cleaning. On the other hand, to maintain a consistent supply of herbs such as basil may require seeding a new crop only every two or three months. Crops that can be harvested multiple times, sometimes called cut-and-come-again, are capable of providing frequent harvests with minimal maintenance.

Life cycle also affects the difficulty to maintain crop health. Growing a healthy tomato crop requires maintaining the growing system at an appropriate EC, pH, and climate for several months. This is a long period during which there could be potential mistakes. The time available for a microgreen crop to experience problems is only a few weeks at most.

LIGHT REQUIREMENT

A crop's light requirement is the amount of light it needs for healthy growth, not the amount of light required to simply keep that crop alive. Even if the light levels in a hydroponic garden do not meet the target light levels for a crop, it does not mean that that garden is incapable of growing that crop, but it is important for a gardener to have appropriate expectations for a crop's performance.

CLIMATE

Similar to a crop's light requirement, there is some flexibility around a crop's recommended climate. A crop can often tolerate suboptimal air temperature, humidity, airflow, carbon dioxide levels, or water temperatures, but when multiple aspects of a climate are simultaneously suboptimal it can be very difficult for a crop to tolerate the collective effects.

Not all fish can tolerate aquariums without mechanical aeration and not all plants can tolerate a hydroponic garden without aeration.

PLANTS AND OXYGEN

One of the first biology lessons students learn is that plants take in carbon dioxide and release oxygen. A potential conclusion one may reach is that plants do not require oxygen to function, but just like humans, plants definitely need oxygen. Plants release oxygen from their leaves but their roots take in oxygen from their surroundings to perform vital functions such as the uptake of water. One of the most common ways gardeners kill plants in a traditional soil garden is over-watering. It can be very confusing to see a plant wilt when sitting in a heavily watered pot, but the wilting is not due to a lack of *water*—it is due to a lack of *oxygen*. Over-watering creates an environment very similar to hydroponics so what's the difference? In hydro-ponics equipment often aerates the water or circulates it in a way to increase the amount of oxygen dissolved in the water. Some hydroponic gardens do not have any aeration equipment and provide oxygen to the roots by positioning a portion of the roots above the water. Some hydroponic gardens provide oxygen to the roots the same way a traditional garden does, by leaving enough time between irrigation events for the root zone to dry out, allowing air to return to areas around the roots to refresh the oxygen supply.

HYDROPONIC SYSTEMS

This section includes build guides for a wide range of hydroponic garden designs. The table below is a quick summary of each system for reference.

KEY

Number References: 1 Low, 5 High

Crop Options:

 Herbs | Salad Greens | Dwarf Tomatoes | Short Flowers,

 Baby Greens/Microgreens | Seedlings | Mushrooms

SYSTEM	DIFFICULTY TO BUILD	DIFFICULTY TO OPERATE	MAINTENANCE REQUIREMENTS	PRICE	YIELD	ELECTRICAL REQUIREMENT	SOUND	CROP OPTIONS
Suction Cup Planters	1	3	3	2	2	0W	No	
Windowsill Garden	3	2	2	3	3	25W	No	
Salad Bowl	2	2	2	2	2	5W	No	
Stream of Greens	2	1	1	3	5	150W	Yes	
Bar Cart	2	2	2	4	2	51W	No	
Bar Tower	4	3	2	3	1	10W	Yes	
Dinner Table	3	4	3	3	2	36W	No	
Picture Frame	4	2	2	3	2	40W	No	
Corner Shelf	3	2	2	3	3	48W	No	
Lift Top Coffee Table	4	2	2	5	4	116W	Yes	
End Table	5	2	2	3	1	9W	No	
Cabinet Farm	4	3	3	5	3	105W	Yes	
Lettuce Locker	5	5	3	5	4	111W	Yes	
Bathroom Flower Garden	2	2	2	3	1	18W	No	

BUILD DIFFICULTY	PRICE	ELECTRICAL REQUIREMENT	MAINTENANCE REQUIRED	PEOPLE REQUIRED	LIGHT INTENSITY
Low	Low	0 W, 2 AA batteries with optional moisture meter	Moderate	1	Natural light, variable by season and location

SUCTION CUP PLANTERS

THE SUCTION CUP PLANTERS GARDEN is a great way to add a small garden in locations with windows that receive sunlight for several hours per day. There are many off-the-shelf options for suction cup planters. These planters are typically used to hold plants grown in pots with a soil-based potting mix. In this guide we simply replace the soil-based pot with a hydroponic substrate that provides a couple of benefits.

In a soil-based pot it is recommended to remove the plant to a sink or alternate location when watering to allow the water to drain in a contained space. Moving most plants is not a problem but as the plants mature (for example, a dwarf tomato or vining pea plant), this can be increasingly difficult. Replacing the soil-based pot with a hydroponic substrate greatly reduces the potential mess that could occur if the irrigation water continues to drain from the pot and spills out of the container or if the suction cups fail and the pots fall to the ground. The suction cup planters are fairly strong and when properly installed can hold 10 pounds or more, but there are definitely instances in which they fail. I would much rather pick up a few hydroponic blocks than clean up a pile of soil (especially on carpet!).

MATERIALS

Please read through the build guide before purchasing materials.

ITEM	QUANTITY	DIMENSIONS
GROWING CONTAINERS		
Acrylic flowerpot with drainage tray and mounting tapes	1	5.9 in L x 3.9 in W x 5.1 in H
Suction cup shelves	2	12 in L x 4 in W
Alcohol wipes	1	
SUBSTRATE		
Stone wool grow blocks, large	7	4 in L x 4 in W x 2½ in H
Stone wool grow blocks, small	7	1½ in L x 1 ½ in W x 1 ½ in H
OPTIONAL		
2 oz clear plastic short square dessert cups		1½ in L x 1½ in W x 1¾ in H
Bamboo skewers		12 in L
Soft plant ties, garden wire		
4-inch stone wool block cover		4 in L x 4 in W
Thumbtacks		
Coco-cap, 6 inches		6⅖ in L x 6⅖ in W x 1⅘ in H
Moisture sensor meter with digital display		
Plastic squeeze bottle with nozzle tip		

TOOLS

Scissors	Knife	Level	DLI meter (optional)

PREPARATION

1 Ensure the window location is well suited for a garden by reviewing Windows and Natural Light in section 1 on page 11.

2 Check the growing container for leaks by filling with water over a sink.

3 Clean the window's surface with an alcohol wipe.

INSTALL THE GROWING CONTAINERS

1 Follow the installation instructions for the specific suction cup growing container you select. Two different growing containers are shown in this design. One of the growing containers uses suction cups to adhere to the window and the other utilizes mounting tape.

2 Use a level when installing the containers to ensure irrigation water does not pool on one side, which potentially could overwater some plants and underwater others.

3 Firmly press suction cups and mounting tape to remove any air bubbles. Check the suction cups every couple of months and press out any air bubbles.

SITE SELECTION

This window garden relies solely on sunlight as there is no grow light included in the design. The success of this garden depends on proper site selection to ensure the light requirements of the plants can be met with the available sunlight. A small DLI meter, such as the one shown in this image, can record light levels over a 24-hour period and provide a measurement that can be compared to recommended DLI ranges for popular hydroponic crops, which are found in the Crop Selection Charts in the appendix on page 177.

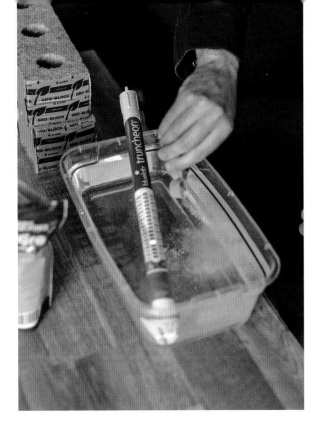

ADD THE HYDROPONIC SUBSTRATE AND PLANTS

There are many substrate options that work well in suction cup planters. I tested several stone wool and coco coir options and all worked well. My favorite substrate for these is a larger stone wool block as it holds more water, reducing the irrigation frequency. Large coco coir blocks work great as well but they are a little messy, which is not ideal for my window located very close to a couch.

1 For stone wool blocks, start by soaking them in a nutrient solution made with a standard hydroponic fertilizer.

2 Allow the blocks to drip off excess nutrient solution before moving them to planters.

IMPORTANT REMINDERS

➔ The most reliable way to determine if it is time to irrigate stone wool or coco coir blocks is by lifting the blocks to see if they feel light, which indicates that they are ready to be irrigated. Touching the surface of a block to see if it feels dry is also an option but sometimes it can be difficult to determine if a block feels cold or if it is indeed wet.

➔ The success of a suction cup window garden is directly tied to the location selected. A window with low light levels or extreme temperatures is a challenging location for most hydroponic crops, and the garden may be limited to growing a short list of very hardy low-light crops. Examples of hardy low-light crops can be found in the Crop Selection Charts in the appendix on page 177.

POSSIBLE DRAWBACKS

System may require multiple irrigations per week and frequent checks for moisture levels. This is not a set-it-and-forget-it garden.

ADD-ONS

BLOCK COVERS: Plastic block covers made for stone wool blocks help retain moisture in the block and minimize algae growth on block surfaces. The surface of a wet stone wool block is a prime location for algae growth but by blocking light on the surface of the block, algae growth can be nearly eliminated.

COCO CAPS: Coco caps can also be used as block covers. The rigid coco caps also work great as walls around the blocks to hide the block wrapper. A coco cap wall gives a more natural look to the garden and can reduce algae growth along the sides of the block if the block wrapper is removed.

SUPPORT STAKES: There are many options for stakes including bamboo, cooking skewers, and chopsticks. Directing crop growth with plant stakes is a great way to avoid overcrowding and improve airflow in a tightly pa cked suction cup garden.

MOISTURE SENSOR: This moisture sensor meter with digital remote display can make it much easier to determine when to irrigate this garden. There are many moisture meter options with trade-offs to each. To learn more about moisture meters visit www.farmertyler.com/homehydroponics/moisturemeters

PLASTIC SQUEEZE BOTTLE WITH NOZZLE: Precise irrigation of the suction cup window garden is much easier when using a squeeze bottle with a nozzle tip. Direct the nutrient solution into exposed areas of growing substrate or subirrigate the planters by adding nutrient solution to the planter shelf. Track the amount of nutrient solution required to completely irrigate the garden using the measurements on the side of the squeeze bottle. Prepare one to two weeks of nutrient solution in advance and store it in the squeeze bottles in a cool, dark location. Mixing nutrient solution in advance can greatly reduce the required maintenance time for this garden.

Add-ons such as block covers, support stakes, moisture meters, and DLI meters can transform a simple suction cup window planter into a high-tech hydroponic garden.

THE NUTS AND BOLTS OF MAINTENANCE

IRRIGATION: Follow the Drain-to-Waste or No Reservoir and No Leachate irrigation strategies detailed in section 4 on pages 164 and 165.

PLANTING: Start seedlings directly in the garden or transplant seedlings started elsewhere.

SUITABLE CROPS: The crops suitable for this garden depend on the specific installation location. Windows receiving full sun for many hours per day may provide enough light for dwarf fruiting crops while windows that receive no direct sunlight may only be capable of growing microgreens. It is also important to consider the height limitations of the crop in this garden, which will depend on the specific spacing used between planters. This garden may not be well suited for top-heavy crops.

SOIL-BASED OPTION: Use traditional soil-filled garden pots and place them on the suction cup planter shelf. Remove the garden pots when watering to allow them to drain elsewhere before returning them to suction cup planters.

3 Move the stone wool blocks into the planters. If the block does not fit into the planter it may be necessary to remove the wrapper and cut the block to fit. It is easier to cut stone wool after soaking it but cutting before soaking is also possible.

4 Seedlings can be started directly in the suction cup planters using a small transparent cup as a humidity dome or seedlings can be started elsewhere and transplanted into the stone wool blocks. See Propagation in section 4 on page 157 for more information on the various ways to start seedlings.

BUILD DIFFICULTY
Moderate

PRICE
Moderate

ELECTRICAL REQUIREMENT
0 W without light, 18 W with optional light, and additional 7.3 W with heat mat

MAINTENANCE REQUIRED
Low to Moderate

PEOPLE REQUIRED
1

LIGHT INTENSITY
Natural light, variable by season and location

WINDOWSILL GARDEN

THE WINDOWSILL GARDEN makes use of free sunlight and the generally underutilized windowsill space. There are many ways to modify this design with optional lights and heat mats depending on your local climate and available sunlight. With its small size this garden may be capable of providing only enough salad greens for one small salad per week. To maximize the value of this garden I recommend using it to grow herbs. This garden is capable of growing microgreens but there are far simpler garden designs better suited for microgreens. This garden can also grow dwarf tomatoes but there may be risk of the tomato plants getting too top-heavy and making the garden unstable on a skinny windowsill.

MATERIALS

Please read through the build guide before purchasing materials.

ITEM	QUANTITY	DIMENSIONS
STRUCTURE		
Poplar hardwood boards	3	24 in L x 2½ in W x ¼ in D
Pond liner	1	Minimum: 26 in L x 9 in W
⅜-inch stainless steel staples	50	½ in W x ⅜ in H
Galvanized angle corner braces	5	2 in x 1½ in x 1⅜ in
Zinc-plated small corner braces, ¾ inch	4	¾ in x ¾ in x ½ in
#6-32 x ½-inch Philips flathead stainless steel machine screws	18	
#6-32 stainless steel machine screw nuts	18	
#6 stainless steel finishing washers	18	
2-inch hydroponic net pot	1	
40mm ping-pong ball, black	1	1.57-inch (40 mm) diameter
Felt pads, furniture feet	6	¾ in x ¾ in
¼-inch PEX tubing (Cut to fill the growing container bottom.)	1	5 ft L x ¼ in inner diameter (⅜-inch outer diameter)
ADD-ONS		
GROW LIGHT		
18 W LED strip light, 18 inches	1	18 in L
Smart Wi-Fi single outlet	1	
GROW LIGHT STAND		
Poplar hardwood board	1	Actual Dimension: 24 in L x 2½ in W x ¼ in D
Poplar hardwood boards	3	24 in L x 1½ in W x ¼ in D
Hardwood square dowels	2	24 in L x ¾ in W x ¾ in D
Zinc-plated small corner braces ¾-inch	7	¾ in x ¾ in x ½ in
#6-32 x ½-inch Philips flathead stainless steel machine screws	16	
#6-32 stainless steel machine screw nuts	18	
#6 stainless steel finishing washers	16	
1½-inch zinc-plated flat corner braces	2	
#6-32 x ½-inch stainless steel screw	8	
3/16 in x 1 in metallic stainless steel fender washers	2	
#6-32 stainless steel wing nuts	2	
#6-32 x 1½ in stainless steel machine screws	2	
Felt pads, furniture feet	4	¾ in x ¾ in
HEAT MAT		
Windowsill heat mat, 7.3 W	1	20 in L x 3 in W
Digital temperature controller for heat mats	1	

OPTIONAL PAINTING MATERIALS

12oz flat white general-purpose spray paint	2

TOOLS

Drill	⁵/₃₂-inch drill bit	Staple gun	*Wood saw (circular, table, or handsaw)	Measuring tape
⁵/₁₆-inch wrench	Wood clamps	Carpenter pencil	(Optional) Router with plunge base, edge guide, and ¼ in x 1 in router bit	Scissors

*It may be possible to build without a saw if the wood can be precut when it's purchased.

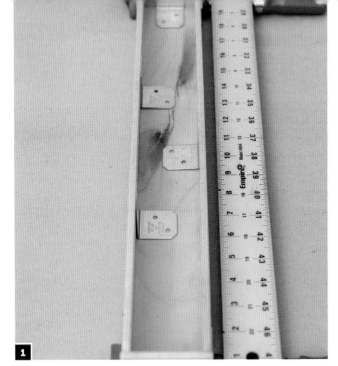

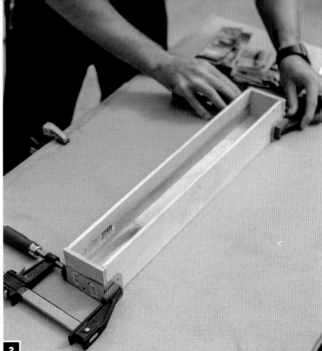

STRUCTURE

This design was built using wood with the following dimensions.

WOOD	QUANTITY	DIMENSIONS
BASE		
Poplar hardwood boards	3	20 in L x 2½ in W x ¼ in H
Poplar hardwood boards	2	3 in L x 2½ in W x ¼ in H
LIGHT BOX		
Poplar hardwood board	1	22 in L x 2½ in W x ¼ in H
Poplar hardwood boards	2	22½ in L x 1½ in W x ¼ in H
Poplar hardwood boards	2	2½ in L x 1½ in W x ¼ in H
LIGHT LEGS		
Square dowels	2	21 in L x ¾ in W x ¾ in D
Hardwood square dowels	2	3 in L x ¾ in W x ¾ in D

BUILDING THE BASE BOX

1 Position all of the base segments (whose dimensions are listed in the table) into position and hold in place with wood clamps. Placing 90-degree braces on the outside of the box can help ensure the angles are square when they're held in place with wood clamps. The sides of the box are positioned on the outside of the base, not on top. With all of the components in place, the dimensions of the base box are 20½ in L x 3 in W x 2½ in H.

2 Position five galvanized angles in the bottom of the base box. More angles can be added if desired, but I found this setup is more than sufficient for holding the structure together. These angles have four holes for screws, but the structure can hold its shape using only two of the four holes. Be mindful that the location of the braces will determine the location of screws visible from the outside of the growing container.

3 Mark the angle locations with a pencil. Also mark each board to indicate the top, bottom, and positioning within the box structure to facilitate the reassembly of the box after drilling marked locations of holes in the angles.

4 Position a small angle at the top of each corner of the box and mark the location with a pencil.

5 Drill ⁵⁄₃₂-inch holes at each of the marked locations.

6 Reassemble the box, securing the angles in position with ½-inch machine screws, machine screw nuts, and finishing washers. Finishing washers on the outside of the box not only improve the box aesthetics, but they also reduce how far the machine screws protrude into the box, reducing the risk of the screws tearing the rubber pond liner on the box's interior.

7 Painting the Windowsill Garden is optional. This garden was painted using multiple light coats of flat white general-purpose spray paint.

8 Add felt pads to the bottom of the growing container to protect the windowsill from scratches.

9 Install the pond liner. See the Bar Tower project in section 3 on page 66 for a detailed guide on installing a pond liner.

10 Build a water-level float indicator using a 2-inch net cup and ping-pong ball.

BUILDING THE OPTIONAL LIGHT BOX

Depending on the window location selected, it may not be necessary to use a grow light. The grow light structure detailed here also works great with the Bathroom Flower Garden project in section 3 on page 150.

1 Position all of the light box segments (whose dimensions are listed in the table) into position and hold in place with wood clamps. Placing 90-degree braces on the outside of the box can help ensure the angles are square when held in place with wood clamps. The 22½ in L x 1½ in W sides of the box are positioned on the outside of the 2½-inch-wide base. With all of the components in place, the dimensions of the light box are 22½ in L x 3 in W x 1½ in H.

2 Position a small angle in each of the four corners of the light box and three small angles along the length of the box holding the sides to the top of the box.

3 Lift and hold the small angles positioned in the box corners and then mark the hole locations with a pencil.

4 Mark each board to indicate top, bottom, and positioning within the box structure to facilitate reassembly of the box after drilling marked locations.

5 Drill ⁵⁄₃₂-inch holes at each of the marked locations.

6 Reassemble the box securing the angles in position with ½-inch machine screws, machine screw nuts, and finishing washers.

7 Mark locations for light mounts on the top 22 in L x 2½ in W x ¼ in H board. The light mounts are located at the 7⅜-inch and 14¾-inch positions along the 22½-inch length of the top board.

8 Drill ⁵⁄₃₂-inch holes at the marked locations for the light mounts.

9 Install the light mounts with ½-inch machine screws and machine screw nuts. The nuts are positioned on the top of the light box.

10 Drill ⁵⁄₃₂-inch holes in the middle of the short sides of the light box.

11 Assemble the light legs by attaching the 3 in L x ¾ in W x ¾ in D board to the end of the 21 in L x ¾ in W x ¾ in D board using a 1½-inch corner brace and ½-inch screws.

8

PROJECT ADD-ONS

→ Window locations can experience temperature extremes more than other locations in a home. In cold climates it may be beneficial to add a heat mat with a thermostat to maintain a root zone temperature warm enough for germination and healthy crop growth. A 20 in L x 3 in W windowsill heat mat fits perfectly under this garden.

→ A small fan is always a great addition to an indoor garden. Visible leaf movement is an indication that the fan is providing sufficient airflow.

12 The light box connects to the light legs with 1½-inch machine screws, ³⁄₁₆ in x 1 in fender washers, wing nuts, and finishing washers. There are two ways to create holes in the light legs to fit the 1½-inch machine screw extending from the light box through the ¾-inch square dowel. The first and easier option is to drill ⁵⁄₃₂-inch holes in the ¾-inch square dowel at desired mounting heights for the light box. The second, and more complicated option, is to create a hole stretching almost the full length of the 21-inch-long light legs using a ¼- x 1-inch straight router bit. The router bit method enables easy adjustment to the height of the light box while the alternative requires detaching the light box from the light legs to adjust the mounting height. Both methods can be used to build a functioning grow light support structure and, truthfully, the height of the light box does not need to be adjusted very frequently so it is not a huge burden simply to detach the light box from the legs to readjust the mounting height.

13 Paint the light box and legs if you choose. This structure was painted using multiple light coats of flat white general-purpose spray paint.

14 Install the grow light into the light mounts.

15 Add felt pads to the bottoms of the light support legs.

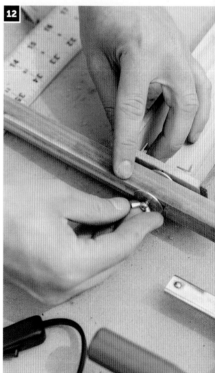

12

SUBSTRATE SELECTION

This garden does not have a drain, which creates the potential for overwatering and drowning plant roots. The primary substrate used in this garden is stone wool and while it is quick-draining and designed for hydroponics, it is not designed to sit in stagnant water. To avoid drowning plants growing in stone wool it is important to provide space under the stone wool for excess irrigation to drain. As plant roots extend out of the bottoms of the stone wool cubes, they can access the nutrient solution pooling below, but it is important to minimize the amount of time the stone wool cubes themselves sit in stagnant water. The stone wool cubes can be lifted off the lower surface using expanded clay pellets, washed river rocks, marbles, PVC pipes, or any other clean hard object that will not rot and retains minimal moisture. Organic substrates such as coco coir chips and wood bark can also be used to lift the stone wool cubes off the lower surface but over time they will rot and, unlike the options already described, organic substrates used below the stone wool cubes are difficult to wash and reuse. Of the many options tested for lifting the stone wool cubes, my favorite is hard ⅜-inch outer diameter tubes cut into 1- to 2½-inch segments. These small blue tube segments are inexpensive, easy to wash/reuse, and maximize the space for excess irrigation to drain below. I also like that these tubes are low profile, which minimizes the amount of exposed stone wool cube protruding from the top of the windowsill garden box.

STARTING AND OPERATING THE GARDEN

1 Fill the bottom of the garden box with one of the recommended substrates (see above). This garden has approximately forty 1½-inch-long segments of ⅜-inch outer diameter tubing.

2 Add transplants or start seedlings directly in the garden. To start seedlings in the garden, begin by soaking the stone wool cubes in a hydroponic nutrient solution. Add seeds to the cube surfaces (see the Crop Selection Charts in the appendix on page 177 for recommended number of seeds per cube for popular hydroponic crops). Add humidity domes and/or mist the surfaces of the stone wool cubes daily until the seeds germinate.

3 For the first two weeks, irrigate the box by adding hydroponic nutrient solution directly to cube surfaces. Two weeks is sufficient for most crops to extend their roots below the cube to access the nutrient solution pooling below.

POSSIBLE DRAWBACKS

The roots of the plants in this garden will likely entangle with neighboring plants, making it difficult to remove and replace individual plants without damaging others.

4 Use the ping-pong ball and net cup to monitor the water level in the garden. Fill the bottom of the garden with a hydroponic nutrient solution up to the point where it comes to contact the bottoms of the stone wool cubes. Add the ping-pong ball to the net cup and note the height at which the ball floats; this is the target fill height for future irrigations. Irrigate the garden whenever the ping-pong ball is no longer floating. Depending on location and crop maturity, the irrigation frequency could be as little as once per week or as often as daily for large, fast-growing crops.

5 After the first two weeks, add nutrient solution directly on top of the ping-pong ball in the net cup and stop once the ping-pong ball reaches its target float height as determined in step 4.

THE NUTS AND BOLTS OF MAINTENANCE

IRRIGATION: Follow the Reservoir Management or No Reservoir and No Leachate irrigation strategies (see section 4 on pages 164 and 165). This garden is unique in that it has multiple viable irrigation strategies.

PLANTING: Start seedlings directly in the garden or transplant seedlings started elsewhere.

SUITABLE CROPS: The crops suitable for this garden depend on the specific installation location and on the use of the optional grow light. Windows receiving full sun for many hours per day may provide enough light for dwarf fruiting crops while windows that receive no direct sunlight may only be capable of growing microgreens. This garden may not be well suited for top-heavy crops. A tall crop may become so top-heavy that it tips over the Windowsill Garden.

SOIL-BASED OPTION: Use traditional soil-filled garden pots and place them in the Windowsill Garden. Remove the garden pots when watering to allow them to drain elsewhere before returning them to the Windowsill Garden.

BUILD DIFFICULTY	PRICE	ELECTRICAL REQUIREMENT	MAINTENANCE REQUIRED	PEOPLE REQUIRED	LIGHT INTENSITY
Low to Moderate	Low to Moderate	5 V USB outlet (2.5 W–5 W)	Low to Moderate	1	100–150 umol/m2/s

SALAD BOWL

THE SALAD BOWL GARDEN is one of my favorites! It is small, easy, reliable, and pretty. The major challenge with this garden is finding the perfect materials to build it. I tested several bowls, plates, lights, and supports for the light before landing on the ones detailed in this design.

MATERIALS

Please read through the build guide before purchasing materials.

BOWL

This system can be built with any bowl and plate, but it is important to ensure the plate diameter allows it to stay fairly high up in the bowl to maximize the amount of space below for nutrient solution. Another option is to allow the plate to rest on a support below (such as a stone wool block) but this increases the chance of exposing the reservoir to light, which could lead to excessive algae growth.

PLATE

Most plastic products have a recycling code that appears as a number between 1 to 7 located in the middle of a triangle. This code indicates the kind of plastic that was used to manufacture the product. It is important to select the appropriate plastic when selecting a plate for this garden. When building this garden, I tested plates made of both poly-

The most challenging part of this design is finding a bowl and plate that fit well together. Additionally, the plate needs to be made of a plastic soft enough to drill without cracking it.

SPECS

GROWING CONTAINERS		
White porcelain bowl, 180 oz	1	12½-inch diameter at top, 5¼ in H
Gray polypropylene (PP) BPA-free plate	1	10½-inch diameter
Hydroponic net cups	4	Outer diameter at top: 2⁵⁄₁₆ in Inner diameter at top: ⅘ in Outer diameter at bottom: ⅔ in Height: 1⁶⁄₁₆ in
SUBSTRATE		
Stone wool grow block	1 block	4 in L x 4 in W x 2½ in H
Stone wool seedling plugs	4 plugs	1 in L x 1 in W x 1⁹⁄₁₆ in H
GROW LIGHT		
LED umbrella plant light, 5 W	1	4⅓-inch diameter, adjustable height
OPTIONAL		
Small fan	1	
2-oz clear plastic short, square dessert cups (optional for starting seedlings directly in the garden)	4	1½ in L x 1½ in W x 1¾ in H
Small air pump with air stone	1	
Water-level indicator buoy	1	3⁷⁄₁₀ in deep 6½ in total height

TOOLS

Drill	⁵⁄₃₂-in. drill bit	Step drill bit	Deburring tool	Knife	Marker
Measuring tape					

The Salad Bowl garden design uses a very low-intensity grow light that will likely produce leggy growth as seen in this lettuce crop. The produce still tastes great, but the leaves are delicate and the stems are elongated.

ethylene terephthalate (PET) and polypropylene (PP). The PET plates shattered when they were drilled but the PP plates were soft enough to drill without shattering.

LIGHT

The grow light I used in this design is the GrowLED Umbrella Plant Grow Light. This grow light is the lowest power grow light shown in any garden design described in this book. At a 4-inch distance from the crop, this light provides 100 umol/m2/s. This grow light also has a built-in timer that automatically runs the light on a 16-hours-on/8-hours-off photoperiod. At a 4-inch distance from the crop this means the plants receive a DLI of 5.76 mol/m2/d. Even

microgreens, one of the crops with the lowest light requirements, has a recommended DLI of 7 mol/m2/d.

The Salad Bowl design can be modified for higher light levels by adding additional lights or using a more powerful grow light. Flexible neck grow lights, such as the one used in the Picture Frame Garden in section 3 on page 82, are often more powerful and could be clipped onto the rim of the bowl. Another option is to use an LED strip light attached to a stand, similar to the setup in the Windowsill Garden in section 3 on page 40.

ASSEMBLE

1 Drill a ⁵⁄₃₂-inch hole at the center of the plate.

2 Mark the location of the plant sites by positioning the center of a square at the center of the plate and marking the four corners. I used the top of a 5 in x 5 in humidity dome I already had on hand, but another option is to use a 4 in x 4 in stone wool block.

3 Drill 1-inch holes at the marked locations using a step drill bit.

4 Clean off any plastic shavings using the deburring tool.

5 Test to see if the net cups fit in the 1-inch drilled holes. If the net cups do not fit, use the deburring tool to slowly widen the holes until the cups fit.

6 Soak the 4-inch x 4-inch stone wool block in a hydroponic nutrient solution using the porcelain bowl or separate container.

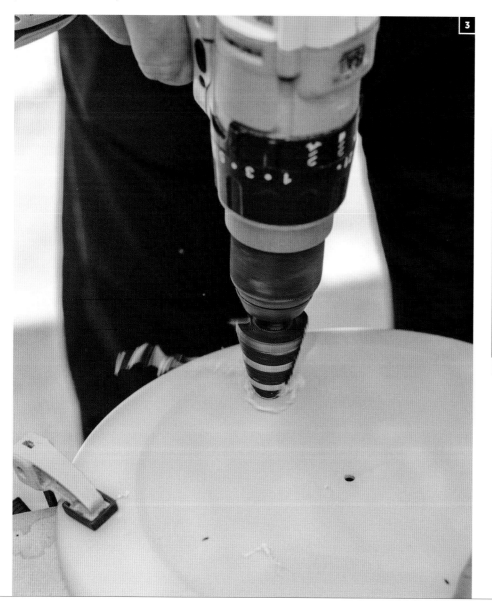

IMPORTANT DETAILS

➡ Gently lift a seedling partially out from its hole to check water depth in the garden. Add additional nutrient solution, which has been premixed in a separate container, to maintain a water level that contacts the bottom of the net cups. As plants mature their roots will extend into the nutrient solution enabling them to tolerate lower water levels, but it is important to maintain a water level that touches the bottoms of the net cups until the plants do mature.

➡ Add a small fan to improve crop growth.

➡ Add a small air pump with air stone if you're planning on growing crops with higher root zone oxygen requirements.

➡ Add a moisture level indicator buoy to quickly check water level without lifting plants. This moisture level indicator is 6½ inches (16.5 cm) tall, enabling it to reach the bottom of the bowl while still positioning the indicator high enough to view.

7 Remove the outer wrapper from the stone wool block and use a knife to slice off some of the top to create a stone wool block measuring 4 in L x 4 in W x 1⅞ in H. It is easier to cut stone wool after soaking it, but it is possible to cut it before soaking as well.

8 Remove the stone wool block. Rinse the porcelain bowl and then fill with 1 gallon water.

9 Thoroughly mix in a hydroponic fertilizer. In this design I use 1 teaspoon of a 10-5-14 ratio per gallon.

10 Position the stone wool block at the center of the bowl.

11 Position the plate to lay flat in the bowl. Rotate the plate as necessary so the plant sites have clearance below and net cups do not contact the stone wool block below.

12 While keeping the grow light upright, insert the grow light's support stake through the center hole of the plate and firmly into the stone wool block below. If the light's support stake does not fit through the center hole use the deburring tool to slowly widen the hole until the stake fits.

13 There are a couple of ways to add plants to this garden.

> ➡ Transplant seedlings that you have started elsewhere. It is best to add seedlings to the net cups outside of the system to avoid pushing down on the plate and misaligning the grow light.

> ➡ Start seedlings directly in the garden. Soak four stone wool seedling plugs in a hydroponic nutrient solution. Remove the net cups from the system and firmly push the plugs into the net cups. Return the net cups with plugs to the garden. Add seeds to the plugs and place small clear plastic cups over each to create a humid environment. Remove the plastic cups after the seedlings germinate.

THE NUTS AND BOLTS OF MAINTENANCE

IRRIGATION: Follow the Reservoir Management irrigation strategy detailed in section 4 on page 164.

PLANTING: Start seedlings directly in the garden or transplant seedlings started elsewhere.

SUITABLE CROPS: Use crops tolerant to low light levels (100–150 umol/m2/s PPFD) that have low root zone oxygen requirements.

14 The grow light will start a 16-hours-on/8-hours-off cycle as soon as it's turned on. Plug the grow light at the specific time you want this cycle to begin. If you're using an alternative grow light in your design, it may be necessary to connect the grow light to a timer or smart Wi-Fi outlet to automate its on/off cycling.

Visit www.farmertyler.com/homehydroponics/productlist to learn more about the specific products used in this garden.

BUILD DIFFICULTY
Low to Moderate

PRICE
Moderate

ELECTRICAL REQUIREMENT
150 W

MAINTENANCE REQUIRED
Low

PEOPLE REQUIRED
1

LIGHT INTENSITY
300–450 umol/m2/s, up to 600 umol/m2/s at 4 inches from lights

STREAM OF GREENS

FLOATING RAFT HYDROPONICS is by far my favorite hydroponic growing method. Plants are grown in rafts floating on a hydroponic nutrient solution. Even as the water level drops over time, plants stay floating at the surface, maintaining their access to the nutrient solution. Floating raft hydroponic gardens require no complicated plumbing and can even operate without electricity when they're placed in a location with adequate natural light. They're reliable, inexpensive, and productive! The drawbacks of a floating

raft garden are its heavy weight and use of Styrofoam™ (polystyrene foam) boards. The use of Styrofoam is widespread both in food production and distribution yet there are many calls for a ban on all Styrofoam products due to its difficulty to be recycled, contribution to worldwide pollution, and potential effects on human health. The U.S. Food and Drug Administration (FDA) has repeatedly evaluated the health impacts of Styrofoam and has consistently deemed it acceptable for use in contact with food. I feel comfortable with using Styrofoam products in a garden but it is definitely a personal decision. Unfortunately, there are not many

easily accessible alternatives to Styrofoam's use in a floating raft garden. There are some commercial HDPE floating rafts, and it may be possible to build a raft out of an HDPE cutting board, but the reduced buoyancy of HDPE compared to Styrofoam may makes it difficult to support a crop.

MATERIALS

Please read through the build guide before purchasing materials.

ITEM	QUANTITY	DIMENSIONS
STRUCTURE		
Whitewood boards	2	¾ in x 5½ in x 8 ft
Pond liner	1	Minimum: 6 ft L x 2 ft W
⅜-inch stainless steel staples	50	½ in W x ⅜ in H
Galvanized angle corner braces	4	2 in x 1½ in x 2¾ in
#9 x ¾-inch stainless steel wood screws	32	
GROWING CONTAINER		
Polystyrene hydroponic seed tray, 128-plug tray	1	26¼ in L x 13½ in W
Polystyrene hydroponic lettuce raft, 28 sites	1	4 ft L x 2 ft W
ELECTRICAL COMPONENTS		
48 W LED strip light, 4 feet	3	4 ft L
Smart Wi-Fi single outlet	1	
Small fan	1	
Submersible water pump, 160 GPH, with venturi attachment	1	

SPECS

PAINTING MATERIALS

General-purpose white interior/exterior multisurface primer, sealer, and stain blocker		1 quart

TOOLS

Wood clamps	*Wood saw (circular, table, or handsaw)	Drill	Staple gun
Electric foam cutting pen tool	Measuring tape	Wood ruler	

*It may be possible to build without using a saw if the wood can be precut when it's purchased.

Floating raft systems are beginner-friendly yet incredibly productive. Their reliability and productivity make them one of the most popular systems for commercial hydroponic farms.

STRUCTURE

This design was built using wood with the following dimensions.

WOOD	QUANTITY	DIMENSIONS
Whitewood board	2	55 in L x 5½ in W x ¾ in H
Whitewood board	2	12⅜ in L x 5½ in W x ¾ in H

BUILDING THE FRAME

To ensure the frame sits flat on the surface at the selected location it may be best to either add a bottom board (not included in this design) or assemble the frame (steps 1 and 2) in the final location.

1 Hold the frame together with wood clamps.

2 Install the angle corner braces.

 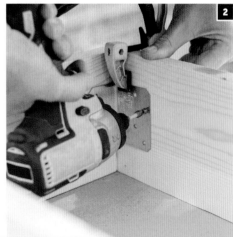

3 Paint the frame if desired. In this design I painted the frame with a general-purpose white multisurface primer, sealer, and stain blocker paint.

4 Once the paint dries, install the pond liner. See the Bar Tower in section 3 on page 66 for a detailed guide on installing a pond liner.

INSTALLING THE GROW LIGHTS

The floating raft garden in this design is positioned under a cabinet. This location provides a surface at an appropriate height above the pond that's perfect for mounting grow lights. If such a location is not available for you, another option is to build a support structure for the grow lights (see the Windowsill Garden on page 40, for example). A grow light mounting height between 8 to 18 inches above the raft surface is suitable for growing most leafy greens and herbs if utilizing grow lights with a light intensity similar to the grow lights detailed in this design.

1 Install the grow light mounts.

2 Install the grow lights into the mounts.

3 Daisy chain the grow lights together and connect the power cable to a smart Wi-Fi outlet.

4 Program the smart Wi-Fi outlet to the photoperiod (on/off times) suitable for selected crops.

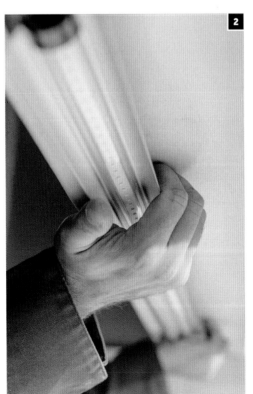

HOW BIG?

Floating raft hydroponic gardens can be designed for nearly any space, but the selected dimensions will have an impact on maintenance requirements and ease of finding materials.

➡ WIDTH AND LENGTH: Pre-manufactured rafts for hydroponics are typically available in 4 ft x 2 ft, 26½ in x 13½ in, or 20 in x 10 in. Building a floating raft garden that easily fits rafts of these dimensions will simplify the building process. Another option is to build custom rafts from large sheets of Styrofoam but this requires cutting and drilling into the foam. See Building Rafts on page 58 later in this guide for tips on customizing raft dimensions.

➡ DEPTH: A floating raft garden can be as shallow as 2 inches but increasing the depth decreases the maintenance requirements. For example, a 5- to 6-inch-deep floating raft garden (as seen in the Stream of Greens design) can grow leafy greens with as little as one refill of the reservoir per month while a 12- to 18-inch-deep floating raft garden may only need a refill once every two months! A deep floating raft garden not only contains more available water for the crop, it helps maintain a stable EC and pH for longer periods of time. The primary drawback of a deep floating raft garden is the significant increase in weight (each gallon weighs over 8 pounds). I do not recommend building a system shallower than 3 to 4 inches.

POSSIBLE DRAWBACKS

This garden generates some noise, which can be annoying. The garden also takes up a lot of counter space and when it's filled with water it is very heavy, making it nearly impossible to move without completely draining it.

An electric Styrofoam cutting tool cleanly slices through Styrofoam, making it easy to make custom raft sizes with smooth edges.

BUILDING RAFTS

The 1 ft x 1 ft rafts in this design were cut from a premanufactured 4 ft x 2 ft raft made for hydroponics. The 11¾ in L x 5¼ in W seedling tray raft was cut from a 26¼ in L x 13½ in W 128 site plug tray. An alternative to using or modifying premanufactured hydroponic rafts is to build them from ¾- to 1-inch-thick polystyrene foam insulation board. Cut the foam board with either a knife, saw, or electric Styrofoam cutting tool and then use a step drill bit to create plant sites sized appropriately for the selected hydroponic seedling plugs. Use wood clamps to hold a wood ruler along the desired cut lines to create a guide for the Styrofoam cutting tool.

AERATION

Aerating the nutrient solution in a home hydroponic garden is often not a necessity but it can greatly improve crop health, productivity, and expand the viable crop options. Air pumps and pumps with venturi attachments (see the photo below), both great options in the Stream of Greens, push atmospheric air into the nutrient solution, increasing the availability of oxygen to plant roots. Some crops such as lettuce may only show a slight improvement in growth when provided additional root zone oxygen, but other crops, such as arugula and tomatoes, can have dramatic positive responses to increased root zone oxygen levels. Increased root zone oxygen is especially helpful when water temperatures rise as warm water cannot hold as much dissolved oxygen as cold water. I've found it's especially helpful to aerate nutrient solutions for leafy greens when water temperatures rise above 75 degrees F (24 degrees C). That said, I've also grown great-looking lettuce in hydroponic systems with no aeration at water temperatures around 85 degrees F (30 degrees C), but it is definitely more of a challenge and there are limited crops that can tolerate this situation.

A venturi attachment on a pump draws in atmospheric air and mixes it into the water output from the pump. A pump with a venturi attachment can both aerate and circulate the hydroponic nutrient solution, eliminating the need for a dedicated air pump with air stones as used in the Lift Top Coffee Table shown in section 3 on page 108.

THE NUTS AND BOLTS OF MAINTENANCE

IRRIGATION: Follow the Reservoir Management irrigation strategy detailed in section 4 on page 161.

PLANTING: Start seedlings directly in the garden or transplant seedlings started elsewhere.

SUITABLE CROPS: Use crops that tolerate light levels in the range of 300–450 umol/m2/s that have low to medium root zone oxygen requirements.

DIY PROJECT

BUILD DIFFICULTY
Low to Moderate

PRICE
Moderate to High

ELECTRICAL REQUIREMENT
36 W (51 W with optional fan)

MAINTENANCE REQUIRED
Low to Moderate

PEOPLE REQUIRED
1

LIGHT INTENSITY
175–250 umol/m2/s

BAR CART

This garden design is one of the easiest to build, it simply involves mounting grow lights in a bar cart and building a wood box to hide a traditional 10 in x 20 in plastic seedling tray. One of the best features of this design is the flexibility. A 10 in x 20 in plastic seedling tray is a blank canvas for all types of hydroponic and traditional garden designs.

This garden can easily be used to start seedlings, maintain an assortment of herbs, or simply act as a space to keep herb plants purchased from a grocery store alive. I really like having a garden on wheels that can be rolled out during a party so guests can garnish their drinks with fresh celery, basil, mint, shiso, buzz buttons, sorrel, borage flowers, stevia, marigolds, oxalis, or any other edible plant I can find that might pair well with a drink!

MATERIALS

Please read through the build guide before purchasing materials.

ITEM	QUANTITY	DIMENSIONS
STRUCTURE		
White kitchen cart	1	Assembled Dimensions: 36 in L x 18 in W x 34⅓ in H
¼-inch poplar boards	2	22⁷⁄₁₆ in L x 3½ in W
¼-inch poplar boards	2	11⁷⁄₁₆ in L x 3½ in W
Galvanized angle corner braces	4	2 in L x 1½ in W x 1⅜ in H
#6-32 x ½-inch Philips flathead stainless steel machine screws	16	
#6-32 stainless steel machine screw nuts	16	
#6 stainless steel finishing washers	16	
GROWING CONTAINER		
1020 plant tray		21⁵⁄₁₆ in L x 11 in W x 2¹³⁄₁₆ in H
See the Planting Options in this build guide for additional options.		
ELECTRICAL COMPONENTS		
18 W LED strip light, 18 inches	2	18 in L
Outlet timer, smart Wi-Fi plug-in outlet	1	
OPTIONAL		
6-inch fan with clip attachment, 15 W	1	
Cord channels/raceways	2	3½ in L x 1½ in W x ¾ in D
Stemware racks, stainless steel	2 pack	13⁷⁄₁₆ in L
2-oz clear plastic short square dessert cups for starting seedlings directly in the garden (optional)	10	1½ in L x 1½ in W x 1¾ in H
Stone wool block covers	10	4 in L x 4 in W
Thumbtacks (to secure block covers)		
Moisture sensor meter with digital display	1	
Plant moisture sensor (for gardens using coco coir or potting soil)	1	

TOOLS

Drill	Philips screwdriver	⁵⁄₃₂-inch drill bit	*Wood saw (circular, table, or handsaw)	Two wood clamps (minimum length 12 ½ in)
Pencil	⁵⁄₁₆-inch wrench			

*It may be possible to build without a saw if the wood can be precut when it's purchased.

HOW MANY LIGHTS?

This garden can operate with one, two, or three 18 W LED grow lights depending on desired crop selections and crop performance. More lights improve the uniformity of light levels across the garden, minimizing stretchy crop growth along the edges of the garden. With two lights, as used in this build guide, there will be some stretching along the edges of the garden and plants may lean in toward the center of the garden to receive more light but, overall, plant growth is fast and healthy. With one light, the light levels are very uneven across the garden but there still are spots in the garden directly under lights capable of growing most of the same crops that would be possible with two or three lights. If you're using only one light it may be best to reduce the growing space (closer to 20 in L x 5 in W) or rotate crops between edge and center of garden to try to balance the light received by each plant throughout their lifetime in the garden.

BUILDING THE FRAME

1 Assemble the bar cart following instructions provided by the manufacturer.

2 Cut the ¼-inch poplar boards into two 22⁷⁄₁₆ in L x 3½ in W and two 11⅞ in L x 3½ in W boards.

3 On a flat surface, position the boards to form a rectangle and hold them in place using wood clamps. The shorter 11⅞-inch segments should be positioned between the longer 22⁷⁄₁₆-inch segments to allow the structure to be held together with two the wood clamps with a minimum length of 12½ inches. Ensure the edges of wood are flush and the box corners are square.

4 Place the corner braces at the bottoms of each corner in the interior of the box. For a cleaner finished look make sure the long sides of the braces are positioned along the longer segments of wood and the shorter sides of the braces are positioned along the shorter segments of wood.

5 Use a pencil to trace the hole locations in the braces. Remove the braces and label each board using a pencil at the location of the brace to ensure all segments are returned to their correct position after disassembling.

6 Drill ⁵⁄₃₂-inch holes at each of the marked locations from step 5. This size bit creates a hole larger than necessary, but the extra space makes it easier to adjust the positioning of the braces when reassembling to ensure the box sits flat on the bar cart surface.

7 Clean off any sawdust or splintered pieces.

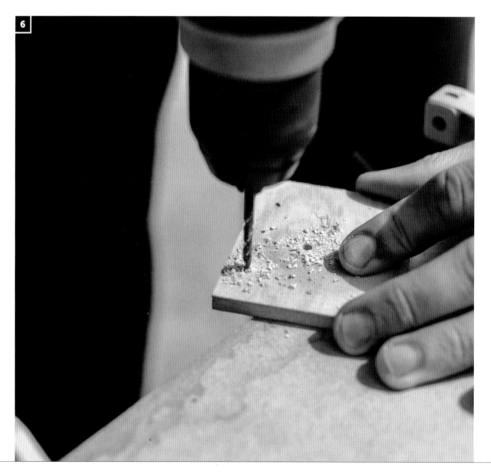

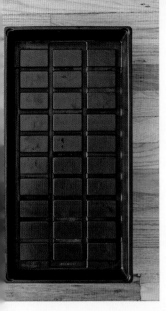

PLANTING OPTIONS

USING A 1020 TRAY: The growing container used in this garden is a heavy-duty cut kit tray measuring 21⅓ in L x 11 in W x 2⅘ in H. There are many trays available with these dimensions. A tray this size is typically called a "1020" based on its typical dimensions of 10 in W x 20 in L. These trays come in various thicknesses and I recommended purchasing a heavy-duty option to reduce the risk of the tray breaking. The specific tray used in this design is classified as a "solid bottom 1020" since it does not have drainage holes, but it is very common for 1020 trays to include drainage holes. One of my favorite ways to grow in these trays is to nest a 1020 with drainage holes into a 1020 without drainage holes. With this setup it is easy to remove the top tray full of plants and dump out any excess irrigation water pooling on the lower tray. Sometimes having some irrigation water on the lower tray is desirable, especially with fast-draining substrates such as burlap for microgreens. See Starting Microgreens in section 4 on page 182 for examples of growing microgreens in a 1020 tray. See Propagation in section 4 on page 157 to see some ways to start plants in a 1020 tray. To learn more about growing microgreens visit www.farmertyler.com/homehydroponics/microgreens

➡ **SHALLOW FLOATING RAFT:** A shallow floating raft is one of the easiest low-maintenance ways to grow hydroponically. A floating raft seedling kit, such as the one seen in Propagation in section 4 on page 157, can be used for extended growth past the seedling stage. The primary issue with longer-term growth in a floating raft for seedlings is overcrowding of plants but simply removing some of the plugs from the board means it is possible to give plants more room to grow to full maturity. It is important to maintain some nutrient solution in the tray at all times as any roots that grow out of the raft into the nutrient solution below can quickly dry out and die when exposed to open air. An alternative to a floating raft kit is to cut polystyrene sheets to fit the 1020 tray. Sheets should ideally be 1-inch thick to support the weight of plants when lifted out of the garden but it is possible to use sheets as thin as ½ inch. The sheets should be handled with care when lifted to avoid them cracking under the weight of mature plants.

➡ **STONE WOOL BLOCKS:** Stone wool blocks come in many sizes and are a convenient way to grow plants in a soilless garden. Steps for preparing and using stone wool blocks can be found in the Suction Cup Planters design in section 3 on page 34.

➡ **COCO COIR BLOCKS:** Coco coir blocks are a great alternative to stone wool and are very forgiving to new growers. Coco coir retains lots of moisture, enabling it to go many days without irrigation when you're growing small plants (depending on environmental conditions). While able to retain a lot of moisture, coco coir is also difficult to overwater as it can quickly drain off excess. Coco coir can act very similar to traditional potting mixes, making it an easy entry point for growers familiar with traditional gardening who are interested in trying hydroponics.

THE NUTS AND BOLTS OF MAINTENANCE

IRRIGATION: Follow the Drain-to-Waste or No Reservoir and No Leachate irrigation strategies in section 4 on pages 164 and 165.

PLANTING: Start seedlings directly in the garden or transplant seedlings started elsewhere.

SUITABLE CROPS: Use crops that can tolerate low to medium light levels (150–300 umol/m2/s) and are short-growing (maximum height 6 inches).

SOIL-BASED OPTION: Use traditional soil-filled garden pots and place them In the 1020 tray. Remove the pots when you're watering to allow them to drain elsewhere before returning them to the 1020 tray.

POSSIBLE DRAWBACKS

The irrigation with this system is manual, which greatly simplifies the system, reducing potential for mechanical errors, but increases the potential for human error if plants are not checked frequently and irrigated as needed.

Small details such as finishing washers on the exterior of the box not only hide the screw heads, they also help hide the DIY nature of the garden by adding a little professional touch. I've not had any friends ask where I bought the box used in my bar garden, but I know they are thinking it— well, I think they are thinking it!

8 Assemble the box by connecting one corner at a time with a corner brace, ½-inch machine screws, finishing washers, and screw nuts. The finishing washer should be placed on the exterior of the box with the head of the screw. The screw nut should be placed on the interior of the box. Do not fully tighten yet.

9 After attaching all corners of the box, return the box to a flat surface to ensure it sits flat. If necessary, loosen and adjust any corner braces. If the box does not sit flat, it may be necessary to use drill bit to expand the size of the drilled holes to allow more adjustment of corner brace locations. Use a ⁵⁄₁₆-inch wrench and Philips screwdriver to tighten once you're satisfied with the structure of the box.

10 Install grow lights using the mounts included with light. See the How Many Lights? sidebar for options for mounting locations based on desired growth.

11 Connect lights together with link cords and plug into smart Wi-Fi plug-in outlet or other outlet timer to control the light cycle in the garden. Program the outlet or timer to the photoperiod appropriate for the selected crops.

ADD-ONS

This garden design leaves a lot of room for add-ons! The basic build includes building a box and adding lights; once that's complete, there are many options to improve both the aesthetics and overall functionality of the bar cart.

FANS: This garden can operate without a fan, but crop growth will improve with the addition of a fan. Air movement over a crop can help strengthen the plants and keep them compact. Air movement can also help remove pockets of high humidity surrounding plant leaves that can inhibit transpiration and slow plant growth.

SMALL CLEAR PLASTIC CUPS: As shown in several of the build guides in this section, small plastic cups are great for starting seedlings directly in a garden. Place a cup over newly planted seeds to create a high humidity environment that promotes germination. The cups can remain on the seedlings until leaves emerge.

STONE WOOL BLOCK COVER: These covers help prevent algae growth on the surfaces of stone wool blocks. The recipe for algae growth is the presence of algae, light, and nutrients. It is very difficult to completely prevent algae from entering a garden, and it is impossible to grow plants without nutrients, so the best option for controlling algae is not to allow light to hit wet nutrient-rich surfaces that can grow algae. Block covers will naturally flatten out on the stone wool block but thumbtacks can help secure them in place.

CORD COVER: A cord cover channel or cord cover raceway is a great way to organize and hide power cords. In this garden I use two 3½-inch-long segments to conceal the power cord supplying and connecting the grow lights.

BUILD DIFFICULTY	PRICE	ELECTRICAL REQUIREMENT	MAINTENANCE REQUIRED	PEOPLE REQUIRED	LIGHT INTENSITY
Low to Moderate	Moderate	9.5 W	Low to Moderate	1	50 umol–650 umol, variable with natural light

BAR TOWER

VERTICAL AEROPONIC TOWERS can look awesome but they can be one of the more challenging hydroponic systems to operate. This design aims to minimize some of those challenges by using a relatively simple aeroponic irrigation design and hardy crop selection.

MATERIALS

Please read through the build guide before purchasing materials.

ITEM	QUANTITY	DIMENSIONS
STRUCTURE		
Wood wine/liquor boxes	2	3¾ in L x 3½ in W x 12¼ in H
½ in x 4 in x 4 ft weathered hardwood boards	2	Actual Dimensions: 3⅞ in W x 4 ft L x ⅜ in thick Dimensions may vary slightly for each board due to the natural characteristics of weathered hardwood boards.
Plywood panel, ¾ inch thick	1	11 in L x 7 in W x ¾ in H
Wood sealer for garden boxes	1	1 gallon
Pond liner	1	Minimum: 2 ft L x 2 ft W
140 10 mm ⅜-inch stainless steel staples	50	½ in W x ⅜ in H
1½-inch black furniture-grade PVC table screw cap	1	
1½ in x 5 ft black furniture-grade schedule 40 PVC pipe	1	Outside diameter: 1¹⁴⁄₁₆ in Inside diameter: 1¹⁰⁄₁₆ in
1½-inch plastic pipe cap	1	
Galvanized angle corner braces	6	2 in x 1½ in x 2¾ in
#6-32 x ½-inch Philips flathead stainless steel screws	48	
#6-32 x ¾-inch Philips flathead stainless steel machine screws	2	
#6-32 x ¾-inch Philips flathead stainless steel screws	2	
Hydroponic net cups	6	Outer diameter at top: 1⁵⁄₁₆ in Inner diameter at top: 1¹³⁄₁₆ in Outer diameter at bottom: 1¹⁰⁄₁₆ in Height: 1⅜ in
Clear food contact-safe silicone sealant	1	2.8 fl oz
Foam plugs	12	1 in L x 1 in W x 1 in H
IRRIGATION		
Short cycle timer (adjustable recycling timer)	1	
Submersible water pump, 160 GPH	1	
½-inch black vinyl irrigation line	1	25¼ in L
360-degree spray nozzle with ¼-inch fittings	7	
Zip tie	1	

TOOLS

Wood saw (circular, table, or handsaw)	Jigsaw with scrolling wood blade	Step drill bit	2-inch hole saw	⁵⁄₆₄-inch drill bit
Wood clamps	Staple gun	Sandpaper	Drip irrigation tubing hole punch and fitting insertion tool for ¼-inch emitters	Deburring tool
PVC pipe cutters	Scissors	Drill		

STRUCTURE

WOOD	QUANTITY	DIMENSIONS
BASE		
¾-inch plywood		11 in L x 7 in W x ¾ in H
T-2 SIDES		
½-inch weathered wood boards	2	11 in L x 4 in W x ½ in H
½-inch weathered wood boards	2	8 in L x 4 in W x ½ in H
TOP		
½-inch weathered wood boards	2	12 in L x 4 in W x ½ in H

BUILDING THE FRAME: PART 1

1 All the wood pieces in this build were pretreated with a wood sealer for garden boxes. This step may not be necessary, but I wanted to ensure the wood would be protected from moisture. If you plan on treating your wood with a sealant, I do not recommend doing this before assembly; rather, wait till all components are together and then apply a coat of garden-friendly wood sealant prior to installing the pond liner.

2 Position the 11 in L x 4 in W x ½ in H segments of weathered wood along the 11 in L sides of the ¾-inch plywood and position the 8 in L x 4 in W x ½ in H segments of weathered wood along the 7 in W sides of the ¾-inch plywood covering the exposed ends of the 11 in L segments of weathered wood. Use wood clamps to secure the wood pieces in place.

3 Fasten the sides together with the galvanized angles. Fasten the 11 in L sides to the ¾-inch plywood with the galvanized angles.

HOW TO INSTALL A POND LINER

A common feature in many designs detailed in this book is a growing container with a rubber pond liner. There are many ways to install a pond liner and countless guides can be found online, and my preferred method is by no means the only way. The liner can extend over the rim of the box or be secured with staples just below the inner rim (as shown in the guide). Stapling the liner along the top edge or even folding it over the rim and stapling it to the outside of the box can help maximize the potential fill height within the box without risking leaks through the staple holes.

1 Ensure the interior of the box has no splinters or exposed nails that could potentially puncture the pond liner.

2 Center the liner over the box and then push it flat along the bottom surface.

3 Pinch the liner along the length of the box.

4 Secure the pinched liner in place with a single staple.

5 Flatten the liner along the bottom of the box.

6 With the liner pushed flat along the bottom of the box (including into the corners), secure the liner in place along the other length of the box with a single staple.

7 Again flatten the liner along the bottom of the box and then pinch it along the width with the corners of the liner folded inward.

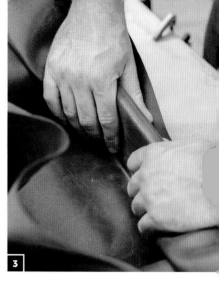

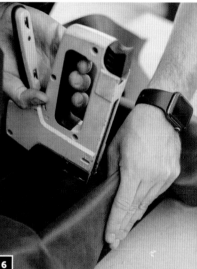

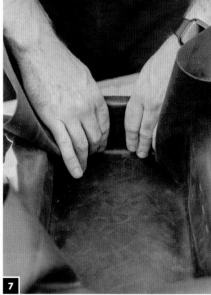

13

14

8 Secure the liner along the width with a single staple.

9 To make the liner easier to work with, it is possible to cut away some of the excess around the corners. Be careful not to cut lower than the rim of the box.

10 Press the fold along the length of the box.

11 Staple the fold in place.

12 Repeat steps 9 through 11 for each corner of the box.

13 Secure the liner in place with staples along the rim of the box.

14 Cut away the excess liner along the rim of the box with a razor blade.

Depending on the box material it may be easier or even necessary to secure the liner with double-sided tape (as shown in the image to the right) instead of staples. The purpose of securing the liner is to hold it in place while filling the reservoir. When the reservoir is full the outward force of the water is generally sufficient to hold the liner in place even if the tape loses its grip on either the liner or the box.

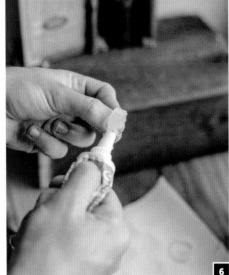

CONSTRUCTING THE TOWER

The towers in this garden are made from schedule 40 furniture-grade PVC pipe that does not contain heavy metals, noxious dioxins, or phthalates. This type of PVC pipe is slightly more difficult to work with as it is not as pliable as standard PVC pipe. To conceal the PVC pipe tower within the old wood beverage boxes it is necessary to select a relatively small diameter pipe. If you do not plan on concealing your PVC pipe in small boxes, I highly recommend using PVC pipe with a wider diameter to increase the crop options within this garden and to permit you to grow crops longer without facing limitations on root space as the crop matures.

1 Cut the PVC pipe to 25½ in L using PVC pipe cutters.

2 Secure the PVC pipe to a worktable with wood clamps.

3 Drill ⅞-inch holes with a step drill bit to create plant sites in the PVC pipe. The plant sites in this design are positioned at the following distances from the top of the tower: 2½ in, 5¾ in, 9 in, 15⅛ in, 18⅛ in, and 21⅛ in.

4 Clean the edges of the holes with the deburring tool.

5 Cut away the bottoms of the six net cups.

6 Apply a thick layer of clear food contact-safe silicone sealant.

7 Secure the net cups into the plant site holes. Wipe away any excess silicone sealant. The net cups should be flush with the surface of the PVC pipe and extend slightly into the interior of the pipe.

POSSIBLE DRAWBACKS

As with most vertical aeroponic gardens, this garden is susceptible to leaks if plugs are improperly placed. Plants in a skinny vertical tower often have roots entangled with neighboring plants, making it difficult to remove and replace individual plants without damaging others. System cleaning requires more disassembly work than most other hydroponic gardens. If pump filter is not cleaned, the emitters may clog and plants could dry out.

IRRIGATION MANIFOLD

1 Cut a 25¼-inch-long segment of ½-inch black vinyl tubing.

2 Fold over the end of the ½-inch tube at 23¾ in L and secure the fold with a zip tie. Cut away excess zip tie.

3 Create holes for ¼-inch emitters using the drip irrigation hole punch. Six holes are along one side of the tube positioned at 1½ inches, 4 inches, 7½ inches, 13½ inches, 17 inches, and 20 inches from the fold created in step 2. One additional hole is positioned on the opposite side of the tube at 1¾ inch from the fold created in step 2. These holes position emitters just above the plant sites.

4 Insert 360-degree spray nozzles into each of the holes punched in step 3.

BUILDING THE FRAME: PART 2

Old wood beverage boxes are a great way to conceal the food-safe PVC pipe aeroponic tower, but they do not serve any critical operational purpose. Some potential modifications to this design could include skipping the addition of beverage boxes to conceal the PVC pipe or concealing the PVC pipe with any decorative exterior frame. An interesting industrial version of this design could conceal the PVC pipe in a larger metal pipe or box.

1 Drill a 2-inch hole through the bottom of the 1½-inch PVC table screw cap.

2 Drill a 2-inch hole through one of the 12 in L x 4 in W x ½ in H weathered wood boards. The center of the hole is 2 inches from the sides along the width and 6 inches from the sides along the length.

3 Secure the 1½-inch PVC table screw cap to the wood segment from step 2, aligning the 2-inch holes in both.

4 Slide the PVC pipe tower into the table screw cap.

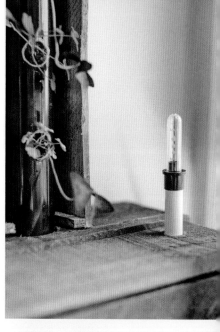

ADD-ONS

→ Drill a ½-inch hole in the lid to install a water-level indicator.

→ A small fan moving air across the face of the Bar Tower garden can help strengthen plant stems and potentially increase plant growth rate.

PLANT SELECTION

The Bar Tower garden is capable of growing a wide range of crops if it's placed in a position with adequate light, but I find this system especially well suited for varieties in plant genus *Oxalis*, commonly known as wood sorrel.

For more information on recommended varieties and planting methods please visit www.farmertyler.com/homehydroponics/oxalis

5 Slide the irrigation manifold into the tower, orienting the folded end closest to the top of the tower.

6 Attach the ½-inch black vinyl tube to the submersible water pump.

7 Cap the top of the PVC pipe with a 1½-inch knock out cap.

8 Move the PVC pipe tower and 12 in L weathered wood board onto the Bar Tower garden base. Position the pump power cord on the least visible side based on the selected location for the garden.

9 Drill ⁵⁄₆₄-inch pilot holes through the four corners of the 12 in L weathered wood board from step 8. Drill deeply enough to penetrate at least ⅛ inch into the Bar Tower base frame.

10 Screw in #6-32 x ¾-inch stainless steel screws (sharp point) into the two pilot holes along the back of the base frame. These two screws secure the lid holding the tower to the base frame.

11 Screw in #6-32 x ¾-inch stainless steel machine screws (flat point) into the two pilot holes along the front of the lid holding the tower. The PVC pipe tower should have a slight angle to encourage water to drain along the back of the tower instead of the front where water might potentially leak out from the plant sites. Adjust the slope of the tower by adjusting the depth of the #6-32 x ¾-inch stainless steel machine screws.

12 With a jigsaw or small wood saw, cut out spaces in the wood boxes for the PVC pipe tower. Make cut-outs in the top and bottom of one box and in just the bottom of the other box. The cut-outs in this design measure 2¼ in W x 2¼ in L.

12

THE NUTS AND BOLTS OF MAINTENANCE

IRRIGATION: Follow the Reservoir Management irrigation strategy detailed in section 4 on page 164.

PLANTING: Root cuttings directly in garden or transplant seedlings started in a separate system.

SUITABLE CROPS: The crops suitable for this garden depend on the specific installation location as this design does not include a grow light.

13 Move the garden to its final location and fill the reservoir with hydroponic nutrient solution.

14 Cover the second half of base frame with remaining 12 in L x 4 in W x ½ in H weathered wood board.

15 Transplant the seedlings or cuttings. Aeroponic gardens such as the Bar Tower are great for developing roots on new cuttings.

16 Connect the pump to the timer and set it to turn on for a few seconds every 30 minutes. The exact on/off times of the pump are flexible. New cuttings benefit from more frequent irrigation while mature crops and seedlings can often thrive with just a few seconds on every few hours! Short "on" times for the pump help reduce the chance of water leaking from the plant sites while still enabling the plants to receive enough nutrient solution to grow.

BUILD DIFFICULTY	PRICE	ELECTRICAL REQUIREMENT	MAINTENANCE REQUIRED	PEOPLE REQUIRED	LIGHT INTENSITY
Moderate	Moderate	36 W	Moderate	1	250–400 umol/m2/s

DINNER TABLE

THE DINNER TABLE AND WINDOWSILL GARDEN designs are all variations of a box with a pond liner. There are so many possible variations to this design, but I find this iteration specifically appropriate for a dinner table due to its low profile and weight-bearing top capable of supporting additional plants, décor, or a spread of condiments. A dinner table is a place for gathering so I wanted to avoid making the garden so tall that it would feel like a barrier or wall segregating the two sides of the table. Balancing the desire to keep the garden short while still including a grow light made it necessary to narrow the suitable crop options for this garden. If a taller garden works well in your specific location, I recommend increasing the height of the garden to expand your crop options.

MATERIALS

Please read through the build guide before purchasing materials.

STRUCTURE

This design was built using ¾-inch-thick reclaimed redwood boards with the following dimensions.

WOOD	QUANTITY	DIMENSIONS
SIDE UPRIGHTS	2	8 in L x 4 ½ in W x ¾ in H
BOTTOM	1	36 in L x 4 ½ in W x ¾ in H
BOTTOM SIDES	2	37¾ in L x 2 in W x ¾ in H
TOP	1	37¾ in L x 4 ½ in W x ¾ in H
TOP SIDES*	2	37¾ in L x 1 ½ in W x ¾ in H

*Alternatively, the top sides could use two 37 ¾ in L x 3 in W x ¾ in H segments. See the build instructions for more information.

POSSIBLE DRAWBACKS

The irrigation with this system is manual, which greatly simplifies the system reducing potential for mechanical errors but increases the potential for human error if plants are not checked frequently and irrigated as needed.

ITEM	QUANTITY	DIMENSIONS
STRUCTURE		
Salvaged redwood boards, ¾ inch thick	3	48 in L x 5 in W x ¾ in H
Wood sealer for garden boxes	1	1 gallon
Super glue gel, cyanoacrylate (*see the build guide; it may not be necessary to use super glue)		
Pond liner	1	4 ft L x 1 ft W
⅜-inch stainless steel staples	50	½ in W x ⅜ in H
Galvanized angle corner braces	10	2 in x 1½ in x 1⅜ in
#6-32 x ½-inch Philips flathead stainless steel screws	40	
#6-32 x 1½-inch Philips flathead stainless steel machine screws	2	
Small rubber bumper pads	8	Diameter: ⅖ in Height: ⅛ in
GROWING CONTAINER		
5- x 5-inch grow trays	14	Top width: 5⅛ in Bottom width: 4¼ in Height: 2¼ in
5- x 5-inch humidity domes	14	Width: 5½ in Height: 2½ in
ELECTRICAL COMPONENTS		
36 W LED strip light, 3 ft	1	
Outlet timer: smart Wi-Fi plug-in outlet	1	

SPECS

TOOLS

*Wood saw (circular, table, or handsaw)	Drill	⁵/₃₂-inch drill bit	Ruler	Paintbrush
Staple gun	Sandpaper	Scissors	Wood clamps	

*It may be possible to build without a saw if the wood can be precut when it's purchased.

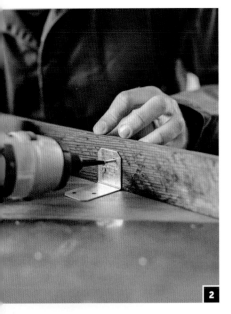

1 Cut the ¾-inch-thick redwood segments for the bottom, bottom sides, side uprights, and top. See the table for specific dimensions.

2 Attach two corner braces to each of the bottom sides. Position the braces at the 12½-inch and 25-inch points along the 37¾-inch length.

3 Attach the two bottom sides to the bottom. The 37¾-inch-long sides should extend ⅞ inch past either side of the 36-inch-long bottom board.

4 Attach one corner brace to each of the side uprights.

5 Attach the side uprights to the bottom board.

6 Install the pond liner. A detailed guide for installing a rubber pond liner can be found in the Bar Tower project on page 66.

7 Originally I made the top sides from two 37¾ in L x 1½ in W segments attached to the top board but I later decided to add an additional 37¾ in L x 1½ in W on top of each of the sides to create a raised lip on the top surface. An easier approach is simply to use 37¾ in L x 3 in W segments instead of two 1½ in W segments stacked on top of each other. Either way, attach the top sides to the top using braces at the 12½-inch and 25-inch locations along the 37¾-inch length (similar to step 2). The top sides should extend at least 1½ inches below the top board to conceal the grow light. In this design the sides extend 1¾ inches below the top board and extend ½ inch above the top surface with the addition of a second 37¾ in L x 1½ in W segment to each side.

8 Install light mounts between the braces on the top board.

9 Attach the grow light to the light mounts.

10 Place the top with the attached light on top of the side uprights.

11 Carefully drill a 1½-inch-deep pilot hole through the top into the side uprights using a $^5/_{32}$-inch drill bit.

THE NUTS AND BOLTS OF MAINTENANCE

IRRIGATION: Follow the No Reservoir and No Leachate irrigation strategy detailed in section 4 on page 65.

PLANTING: Start plants directly in the garden or transplant seedlings started elsewhere.

SUITABLE CROPS: Use crops tolerant of light levels in the range of 250–400 umol/m2/s with a canopy height less than 4 inches.

SOIL-BASED OPTION: Use traditional soil-filled pots and place them in the Dinner Table garden. Remove the pots when watering to allow them to drain elsewhere before returning them to the Dinner Table garden.

The top sides extend ½ inch above the top board to create a raised lip. The sides extend 1¾ inches below the top board to conceal the grow light.

12 Drill in a 1½-inch-long machine screw into each of the pilot holes to secure the top to the side uprights.

13 Attach a power cord to the grow light and connect it to a smart Wi-Fi outlet to program the on/off times.

IMPORTANT DETAILS

→ The substrate selected for use in this garden can have a huge impact on the maintenance requirement. A quick-draining substrate such as a microgreen hemp mat may require a watering every day while a substrate that retains a lot of moisture, such as a fine coco coir, may only need to be watered once per week.

→ This garden can fit seven 5- x 5-inch trays on each level or can accommodate trays of other sizes as long as their bottom width is 4¼ inches or less. This garden operates best when the trays are removed for watering to avoid excess pooling of nutrient solution in the shallow pond liner bottom. I do not recommend placing recently watered trays on the top level as it does not have a liner to retain any nutrient solution dripping from trays. I typically do not place plants on the top level except for special occasions such as a dinner party. See Propagation in section 4 on page 157 for detailed guides on growing microgreens and seedlings in 5- x 5-inch trays.

A Venus flytrap is a fun addition to a dinner table garden.

BUILD DIFFICULTY	PRICE	ELECTRICAL REQUIREMENT	MAINTENANCE REQUIRED	PEOPLE REQUIRED	LIGHT INTENSITY
Moderate to High	Moderate	40 W	Low to Moderate	1 for building process, 2 for wall mounting	100–125 umol/m2/s at base, 250–400 umol/m2/s at 4" from lights

PICTURE FRAME GARDEN

THIS WALL GARDEN is low maintenance, reliable, and beautiful. This garden is not especially productive but it is capable of growing herbs for a quick dining room "harvest and garnish." There are many ways to simplify the assembly of this garden, but I elected for beauty over ease in most building decisions. The result is this is one of the more difficult system builds detailed in this book. For this garden I used 150-year-old redwood

ITEM	QUANTITY	DIMENSIONS
STRUCTURE		
This garden is made from salvaged and weathered boards. Dimensions may vary slightly for each board due to the natural characteristics of weathered hardwood boards. A list of specific board dimensions used in this design can be found in the following step-by-step build guide.		
Salvaged redwood boards, ¾ inch thick	3	48 in L x 5 in W x ¾ in H
½ in x 4 in x 4 ft weathered hardwood boards	6	3⅞ in W x 4 ft L x ⅜ in H Dimensions on these boards varied between 3⅞ in W to 4⅛ in W. The thickness varied between ⅜ inch to ½ inch, but it was generally closer to ½ inch.
Plywood panel, ¾ inch thick	1	20¼ in L x 20⅜ in W x ¾ in H
Wood sealer for garden boxes	1	1 gallon
Pond liner	1	7 ft L x 3 ft W
⅜-inch stainless steel staples	50	½ in W x ⅜ in H
40 x 40 mm stainless steel right angle brackets	20	1⁵⁷⁄₁₀₀ in L x ¹³⁄₁₆ in W x 1 ⁹⁄₁₆ in H, ⅛ inch thick
3 in x 5 in stainless steel L brackets	4	5 in L x ⅘ in W x 3 in H, ¹⁄₁₀ in thick
⅝-inch Philips flathead stainless steel wood screws	42	
#6 x ½-inch Philips flathead stainless steel wood screw (100 pack)	1	
2-inch satin brass mending plates	2	
1-inch satin brass narrow utility nonremovable pin hinge with ¼-inch screws	4	
2⅞-inch heavy-duty wood screws	4	
#8 x 2½-inch wood screws	2	
2-inch net pots	3	
Expanded clay pebbles	10 L	
GROW LIGHT		
Three-bulb plant grow light with 3/6/12 H timer (36 W LED)	1	22-inch flexible arms, 2-inch light 27 inches long including mounting clamp
OPTIONAL		
Cord channel/raceway	1	1½ in W x ¾ in D
Water-level indicator buoy	1	3⁷⁄₁₀ inches deep 6½ inches total height

Note: Weathered wood can have actual dimensions not consistent with these listed dimensions due to the weathering process; those variable dimensions were observed with some boards measuring less than ½ inch thick.

TOOLS

Wood saw (circular, table, or handsaw)	Drill	2-inch hole saw	½-inch hole saw	⁵⁄₆₄-inch drill bit (pilot holes)
Wood clamps	Sandpaper	Ruler	Paintbrush	Stud finder
Scissors				

slats reclaimed from an old grain silo and some weathered hardwood boards from a local home-improvement store. These materials have varying dimensions from board to board requiring small adjustments in cuts while assembling to minimize gaps.

MATERIALS

Please read through the build guide before purchasing materials.

STRUCTURE

This design was built using wood with the following dimensions. I do not recommend cutting all segments before starting! Cut segments as needed to double-check the actual dimensions required to meet the specific purpose for that segment.

WOOD	QUANTITY	DIMENSIONS
¾-inch plywood	1	20¼ in L x 20⅜ in W
½-inch weathered wood	1	13¹⁵⁄₁₆ in L x 1⁵⁄₁₆ in W
½-inch weathered wood	6	13¹⁵⁄₁₆ in L x 4 in W
½-inch weathered wood	2	20¼ in L x 4 in W
½-inch weathered wood	2	21¾ in L x 4 in W
½-inch weathered wood	1	13⅝ in x 3⅞ in W
½-inch weathered wood	1	13⅝ in L x 3½ in W
½-inch weathered wood	1	13⅝ in L x 3⅜ in W
½-inch weathered wood	2	3⅜ in L x 2½ in W
½-inch weathered wood	1	13¹⁵⁄₁₆ in L x 4⅛ in W* *This board was slightly wider than other 4-inch-thick boards
¾-inch redwood	2	21⅞ in L x 4¹³⁄₁₆ in W
¾-inch redwood	2	20¼ in L x 4¹³⁄₁₆ in W
¾-inch redwood	1	13⅝ in L x 3⅜ in W

BUILDING THE FRAME: PART 1

Note: In the following directions, all redwood boards are ¾ inch thick and the weathered boards are ½ inch thick. Use the ⅝-inch stainless steel screws when drilling into ¾-inch redwood or ¾-inch plywood and use the ½-inch stainless steel screws when drilling into the ½-inch weathered wood boards.

1 All wood in this build was pretreated with a garden box sealer. This step may not be necessary, but I wanted to ensure the wood was protected from moisture. If you plan on treating your wood with a sealant, I do not recommend doing this before assembly. Rather, wait till all components are together and then apply a coat of garden-friendly wood sealant.

2 Cut the ¾-inch plywood panel to 20¼ in L x 20⅜ in W x ¾ in H. This is the backboard of the picture frame garden.

3 Cut two 20¼ in L x 4¹³⁄₁₆ in W redwood segments and the two 20¼ in L x 4 in W weathered wood segments. These redwood segments are the side walls of the frame.

4 Attach the 20¼ in L redwood segments along the 20¼ in L edge of the plywood panel. The redwood should be placed along the side of the plywood panel to hide the exposed plywood edge. Secure the redwood to the plywood using a 40 x 40 mm right angle bracket positioned at the center of the 20¼ in L. Before drilling, double-check that the screws are not longer than the thickness of the redwood or plywood boards. If the specific boards used in your garden are slightly less thick it may be necessary to use shorter screws. To improve the strength of the frame, an additional right angle bracket could be used at this step.

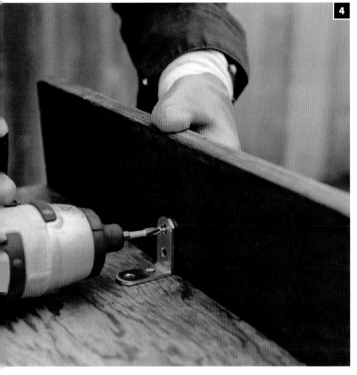

5 Repeat step 4, attaching the other 20¼ in L redwood segment to the other 20¼ in L edge of the plywood panel.

6 Measure the exact length required for the top and bottom redwood segments that will complete the exterior of the frame around the plywood backboard. These segments should cover the exposed edges of the side redwood panels. In this build, these segments measure 21⅞ in L x 4¹³⁄₁₆ in W.

7 Cut two redwood segments to the length measured in step 6. Position these redwood segments along the top and bottom edges of the plywood panel. Measure the total height of the frame including the length of both the side walls and thickness of both top and bottom redwood segments.

8 Cut two 4-inch-wide weathered wood segments to the measurement recorded in step 7. In this specific build these segments were cut to 21¾ in L x 4 in W.

9 The bottom redwood segment attaches to the plywood with four 3 in x 5 in L brackets. Before attaching the bottom, it is important to test the fitting of the other segments already cut. The brackets will be concealed in the side boxes that run along the height of the frame. The 20¼ in L x 4 in W weathered wood segments from step 2 will be positioned to the side of the brackets running parallel to the redwood side walls. The 21¾ in L x 4 in W weathered wood segments from step 8 are the front of the side boxes. After positioning all the pieces, mark the location of the L brackets and remove all the weathered wood segments.

10 Attach the four 3 in x 5 in L brackets to the locations marked in step 9.

11 Attach the top redwood segment along the top exposed edge of the plywood using a 40 x 40 mm right angle bracket. The structure can hold its shape with just one right angle bracket holding the top redwood segment but an optional second right angle bracket can help secure it firmly in position. Position the bracket (or brackets) toward the center of the redwood segments to avoid potentially getting in the way of the boxes that will be positioned on the left and right sides of the frame.

12 Reposition the weathered wood segments from step 9. The 20¼ in L x 4 in W segments should fit between the top and bottom redwood segments; if the fit is too tight it might be necessary to gently hammer the segment into place or shorten the segment. The longer 21¾ in L x 4 in W weathered wood segments will cover the front of the boxes that run along the left and right side of the frame. Adjust the position of 20¼ in L segment until it is flush with the edge of the 21¾ in L segment.

13 Remove the 21¾ in L weathered board segments and position 40 x 40 mm right angle brackets in the interior of the side boxes next to the 40 x 40 mm right angle brackets used to hold the redwood side walls. Mark the location of these brackets on both the plywood and 20¼ in L weathered wood and then remove the 20¼ in L weathered wood.

14 Attach the 40 x 40 mm right angle brackets to the 20¼ in L weathered wood segments and then return the 20¼ in L segments to their previous position from step 12. Attach the other end of the 40 x 40 mm right angle brackets to the plywood. It may be necessary to use a drill bit extender to reach the bracket once it is in position. It is possible to add another bracket to secure the 20¼ in L segment firmly in place but this is optional.

15 Using the 2-inch hole saw, drill a 2-inch hole centered 1¼ inches from the top of the 20¼ in L weathered wood segment on the right side of the frame. This hole can be drilled while the board is still attached to the plywood or it can be removed and drilled.

10

14

16 Measure the distance between the 20¼ in L weathered wood segments running along both sides of the frame. This distance measures 13¹⁵⁄₁₆ inches in my build, but this distance could vary due to variations in weathered wood sizing.

17 Cut a 4 in W segment of weathered wood to the length measured in step 16.

18 Mark the center of the segment cut in step 17 and then drill a 2-inch hole using the 2-inch hole saw.

19 Slide the back of the grow light through the hole drilled in step 17 and through the hole drilled in step 15. The grow light can be difficult to slide through these holes and it may be necessary to detach the 20¼ in L weathered wood segment with the 2-inch hole to smoothly install the grow light.

20 Attach the 13¹⁵⁄₁₆-inch weathered wood segment to the plywood using a 40 x 40 mm right angle bracket. Similar to the side boxes, the top box will also be covered with a 4 in W weathered wood segment. Use a piece of 4 in W weathered wood to position the 13¹⁵⁄₁₆-inch segment to ensure it is close enough to the top of the frame that one piece of 4 in W weathered wood will cover the exposed edges of both it and the top redwood segment.

CONSTRUCTING THE GROWING CONTAINER

1 The growing container sits on the bottom redwood segment between the 20¼ in L weathered wood segments. Measure the distance between the 20¼ in L weathered wood segments to determine the width of the growing container. This should be close to 13¹⁵⁄₁₆ inches, similar to the measurement used for the weathered wood segment that supports the grow light.

2 Cut three weathered wood segments to the measurement recorded in step 1. In my specific build, the weathered wood for this was cut to 13¹⁵⁄₁₆ in L x 4⅛ in W. As mentioned previously, weathered wood dimensions can vary from board to board and this one was slightly wider. These segments will be used for the front, top, and back of the growing container.

3 Cut one redwood segment to the measurement recorded in step 1. This segment will be used for the bottom of the growing container.

4 To maintain a consistent façade on this Picture Frame garden, the front of the growing container has an overhang to hide the edge of the bottom redwood segment. To achieve this while having a level top surface to the growing container, it is necessary to shorten the width of the weathered wood segment that will be used for the back of the growing container. The total amount to shorten the width of the segment can be determined by measuring the thickness of the redwood segment used on the bottom of the frame (in this case, ¾ inch) and subtract that from the width of the weathered wood segments from step 2 (in this case, 4⅛ inches). In this build the backboard of the growing container measures 13¹⁵⁄₁₆ in L x 3⅜ in W.

5 The width of the redwood base also needs to be shortened so the front segment of the growing container will lay flat with the 21¾ inches of weathered wood segments that cover the boxes on the left and right of the frame. The target width of the redwood segment can be determined by subtracting the thickness of the backboard from step 4 from the width of the 20¼ in L weathered wood used to create the boxes for the left and right of the frame. In this case the 20¼ in L segments are 4 inches wide and the blackboard is ½ inch thick, so the redwood board needs to be 3½ inches wide.

6 The left and right sides of the growing container require small segments that fit within the space between the front, bottom, and back of the growing container. In this design that space measures 3½ in W x 2⅝ in H.

7 Cut two weathered wood segments to the dimensions measured in step 6.

8 Position the back, bottom, sides, and front of the growing container into the Picture Frame garden to check that the pieces fit well together.

9 After checking for fit, assemble the growing container using either 40 x 40 mm braces with ½-inch screws or a combination of braces and nails. If you're using thin wood, I recommend making a pilot hole before hammering in a nail to reduce the chance of the wood splitting. This book contains many different ways to assemble growing container boxes (also see the Windowsill Garden, Bar Cart, Bar Tower, or Stream of Greens gardens in section 3), and there are many more methods for making a box that are not included in this book. The important part to remember is the box has a board at the bottom capable of holding the weight of water in the reservoir and there are no protruding nails or sharp edges that could damage the rubber liner that will be added to the growing container.

BUILDING THE FRAME: PART 2

1 Place the growing container into the frame and mark the top edge.

2 Cut the weathered wood segments to cover the exposed plywood behind the grow light and above the growing container. This garden required three segments measuring $13^{15}/_{16}$ in L x 4 in W and one smaller segment measuring $13^{15}/_{16}$ in L x $1\frac{3}{8}$ in W. To make room for the rubber liner in the growing container, the width of the smaller segment should be ¼ inch less than required to reach the marked line for the top of the growing container. Do not attach any of these segments to the plywood; it may be necessary to place screws behind them when mounting the plywood to the wall.

3 Return the growing container to the Picture Frame garden and position the remaining $13^{15}/_{16}$ inches of weathered wood segment on top of the growing container to ensure it fits properly. Adjust the dimensions of the segment as necessary until it easily fits on top of the growing container while the growing container is in its position within the Picture Frame garden.

4 After ensuring the top of the growing container fits, remove the segment and drill three 2-inch holes to hold net cup planters. It is possible to install one, two, three, or even four 2-inch holes for net cups, but I like the aesthetics of three bulbs on the grow light with three plant sites. Plant site spacing for many popular hydroponic crops can be found in the Crop Selection Charts in the appendix on page 177. The centers of left and right plant sites in this design are spaced 3¼ inches from the center of the middle plant site, which is positioned in the middle of the 13¹⁵⁄₁₆ in L growing container top.

5 Sand the edges of the drilled plant sites from step 4 to remove any splinters and test fit the 2-inch net cups into the drill sites. If the net cups do not fit, it may be necessary to sand the edges again to widen the holes.

POSSIBLE DRAWBACKS

Both assembly and installation are challenging. The amount of produce that can be output by this garden is limited by its small size.

6 The grow light connects to its power supply through a skinny plug. This plug can exit the outer frame of the garden through a ½-inch hole. For other grow lights it may be necessary to make this hole larger depending on the size of the power cord. I positioned the ½-inch hole in the frame just to the side of the bottom braces, but the exact position used is flexible.

7 To finish the exterior of the frame there are several options. The 21¾ in L weathered wood segments that cover the left and right sides of the boxes can be attached to the frame using nails, screws, glue, or even magnets. After testing a few options, my preferred method is to add small hinges to the top redwood board connecting to the edge of the 21¾ in L weathered wood segments, making it easy to open up the side boxes to access the light controller or easily access that space when mounting the frame to a wall. Accessing the top box is less critical so it is possible simply to glue or nail the outer cover, but I found it easier to use hinges attached to the top redwood board to secure this segment as well. Depending on preference, you may want to use two 13¹⁵⁄₁₆-inch segments to cover not only the exposed plywood in the top box but also to conceal the grow lights. I attached these two 13¹⁵⁄₁₆-inch segments together using a couple 2-inch mending plates across the width so both segments are supported by the hinges attached to the top redwood board. The hinges used in this design are secured with ¼-inch screws. It is very important to create pilot holes when attaching the braces as it is easy to split either the redwood top board or weathered wood segments when installing screws so close to the edges of the board.

Attaching the side panels to the redwood frame with hinges makes it easy to access the side boxes to program the light controller or drill screws through that section of the backboard into a wall stud when mounting the garden.

ADD-ONS

➜ Use a cord channel to hide the grow light power cord. Use a level when attaching cord channels to the wall to ensure they are straight. The cord channels can be cut to the desired length using PVC pipe cutters.

➜ Add a water-level indicator buoy. The one used in this garden is 6½ inches tall. Drill a ½-inch hole into the top of the growing container to install the water-level indicator.

➜ Net cup covers help reduce the chance of algae developing on the surface of seedlings, which could attract fungus gnats.

MOUNTING TO A WALL

1 This garden can be mounted to a wall using one or preferably two studs. Use a stud finder to locate the center of the studs behind the wall and measure the distance between studs. The studs behind the wall at my home are spaced 16 inches apart, enabling me to mount the 20⅜-inch wide plywood to two studs. Mark the centers of the studs.

2 Drill two #8 x 2½-inch screws into each stud (one in each stud or two in one stud). Use a level and measuring stick to ensure they are positioned at the same height from the ground. Do not fully drill in the screws into the wall; leave approximately 1 inch of the screw outside of the wall.

3 Drill two ½-inch holes in the back of the plywood at the same spacing used when drilling the screws into the wall from step 2. In my garden, the screws in the wall are in studs positioned 16 inches apart. The ½-inch holes in the plywood are positioned 16 inches apart near the top of the Picture Frame garden. The ½-inch holes in the plywood backboard align with the 2 ½-inch screws partially drilled into the wall studs to temporarily support the weight of the garden.

4 Remove all loose wood segments from the garden including the growing container and the 13¹⁵⁄₁₆ in L weathered wood segments covering the exposed plywood behind the grow light. With the help of two people, lift the Picture Frame garden and hang it on the wall by positioning the #8 screws into the ½-inch holes in the plywood. Slowly release the garden to make sure the frame is supported by the #8 screws. The picture frame garden should only rest on these screws temporarily; it is important to further secure the garden to the wall using additional screws.

5 With the garden resting on the #8 screws, check to see if the frame of the garden is level. It may be necessary to reposition the #8 screws or drill additional ½-inch holes in the plywood to make sure garden is level. Once garden is level, use four 2⅞-inch heavy-duty wood screws to secure the plywood to the centers of the studs behind the wall.

FINISHING TOUCHES

1 With the Picture Frame garden securely attached to the wall, the rest of the wood segments and growing container can be returned. It is now safe to attach the 13¹⁵/₁₆ in L weathered wood segments to the exposed plywood behind the grow light using either screws or glue. If you're using screws, it is important to create pilot holes and be careful not to drill too deeply or it may damage the wall behind the plywood. I used quick-drying wood glue to attach the weathered wood segments covering the exposed plywood in my garden.

2 Add a rubber liner to the growing container. See the Bar Tower garden for a step-by-step process to add a rubber liner into a wood box. This garden design uses a thick rubber liner in the growing container, but thinner plastic liners also work.

3 Transplant the seedlings to the net cups. Fill extra spaces in the net cups with expanded clay pellets. Add the net cups to the lid of the growing container.

4 Fill the reservoir with a hydroponic nutrient solution and transplant the seedlings.

THE NUTS AND BOLTS OF MAINTENANCE

IRRIGATION: Follow the Reservoir Management irrigation strategy detailed in section 4 on page 164.

PLANTING: Start seedlings directly in the garden or transplant seedlings started elsewhere.

SUITABLE CROPS: Use crops that can tolerate light levels in the range of 100–200 umol/m2/s that have a low root zone oxygen requirement.

SOIL-BASED OPTION: Place small pots filled with traditional potting mix in the rubber-lined growing container. Remove the pots to water and let them fully drain before returning to growing container.

BUILD DIFFICULTY	PRICE	ELECTRICAL REQUIREMENT	MAINTENANCE REQUIRED	PEOPLE REQUIRED	LIGHT INTENSITY
Moderate	Moderate	48 W	Low to Moderate	1 to 2; the garden requires lifting the shelf (25–50 lb)	275–350 umol/m2/s

CORNER SHELF

ROOM CORNERS ARE GENERALLY an underutilized space; put that space to work with a corner shelf garden! This build requires some drilling and potentially some painting, but otherwise the corner shelf garden is one of the easier hydroponic gardens to build and maintain. This design uses a premanufactured corner bookshelf and off-the-shelf (pun intended!) self-watering pots. This garden may not be the most productive but it can easily supply a constant flow of herbs that can be harvested right next to the dining table. Garnish any meal with fresh herbs just seconds from harvest!

PREPARATION

1 It is easier to drill holes in the middle tiers before assembling the corner shelf, but it is also possible to drill them after assembling the shelf. I did the later as mine was already built and I repurposed this corner shelf into a garden.

2 It is important the shelf has a removable top or bottom, otherwise it may be impossible to slide the grow light into the shelves with drilling an additional hole in the top or bottom.

GROW LIGHTS

1 Mark the spot for drilling through the shelves. I used a 4-inch square stone wool block positioned at the front corner of the shelves to mark a spot 5⅝ inches from the front corner and 4 inches to either side. At this location the grow light is approximately 10 inches from the back corner. I positioned the light here as I wanted some of the space along the front edge of the shelf to still be usable, but I also wanted to position the light at least 6 inches away from the plants. You may want to position the light closer to the front corner to allow the plants to grow larger, but I do not recommend positioning it any farther back as the light may damage the plants when it's positioned too close.

MATERIALS

Please read through the build guide before purchasing materials.

ITEM	QUANTITY	DIMENSIONS
STRUCTURE		
White five-tier wall corner bookshelf	1	11 in L x 11 in W x 65 in H
1-inch boat nails, ring shank, bronze	5	1 in L
Cord cover channel/raceway kit	1	45 in L x 1½ in W x ¾ in D
All-purpose white interior/exterior multisurface primer, sealer, and stain blocker	1	1 quart
GROWING CONTAINER		
Self-watering hanging planters	5	5 in W x 5⁵⁄₁₆ in H
GROW LIGHT		
48 W LED strip light, 4 feet	1	4 ft L
Smart Wi-Fi single outlet	1	
SUBSTRATE		
Expanded clay pebbles	10 L	
Stone wool grow blocks, small	10	1½ in L x 1½ in W x 1½ in H
Optional		
2-oz clear plastic short square dessert cups	10	1½ IN L x 1½ IN W x 1¾ IN H

TOOLS

Drill	2-inch hole saw	Paintbrush	PVC pipe cutter	Hammer
¹⁄₁₆-inch drill bit				

Before drilling check to see if the light will fit within the diameter of the drilled holes. There are many LED grow light bar options that could be used in this design as long as the drilled holes are appropriately sized.

2 Using the 2-inch hole saw, create a 2-inch hole into the middle tier shelves centered at the marked locations from step 1.

3 After drilling check to see if there are any major chips to the paint around the holes. At this point you may want to apply a coat of white paint to cover any exposed particle board.

4 Assemble the corner shelf according to the manufacturer's instructions. Before attaching the top of the corner shelf, slide the grow light through the middle tiers. If it's already assembled, remove the top and then install the grow light. It is important to position the end of the grow light that attaches to the power cord closer to the base. I recommend the SunBlaster grow light because it includes metal clips that attach to the back of the light to make it easier to hang from a chain or rope. In this design the metal clips are positioned just above the surface of a shelf to prevent the light from slipping downward. One of the two metal clips can be seen just above the second shelf from the top. These clips were painted white after assembly.

5 Install the top of the corner shelf.

WEIGHT CAPACITY

The specific corner shelf used in this design is rated only for a 6-pound weight capacity per shelf. The self-watering pots in this garden are large enough to hold one gallon of water, which weighs approximately $8\frac{1}{3}$ pounds. It is important to be mindful of the weight capacity when adding items to these shelves or deciding how much water you want to add to a pot. The recommended fill height for water when using these pots for a traditional potting mix is only $\frac{2}{5}$ inch; this is less than $\frac{1}{10}$ of a gallon. By using stone wool and expanded clay pellets it is possible to maintain a higher water level without waterlogging the crop, but be mindful of the weight of water as it is easy to surpass the weight capacity per shelf.

6 Move the corner shelf to its final position and secure it to the wall.

7 Connect the power cord to the grow light. Use the PVC cutter to cut segments of cord raceway to hide the power cord.

8 Connect the power cord to a smart home wi-fi outlet and program light schedule. I use a 12-hours-on/12-hours-off cycle with this garden.

SELF-WATERING POTS

1 Test how you want to position and space the pots on the shelves. To reduce the weight directly on the shelves it is best to position the pots in locations at which they can be attached to the vertical supports.

2 Mark the locations for hanging the pots.

3 Use a ¹⁄₁₆-inch drill bit to create small pilot holes at the marked locations from step 2.

4 Use a nail, screw, or hook that enables easy removal of the growing containers. I originally used hooks in this design but I eventually replaced them with bronze nails as it was much easier to remove growing containers from a straight nail compared to a hook.

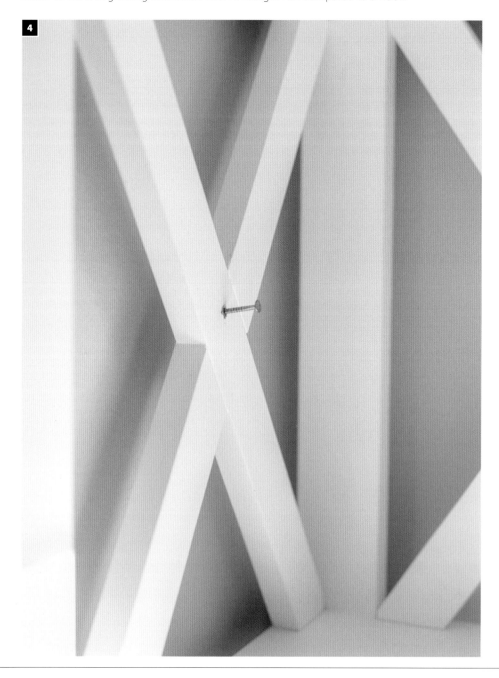

There are many versions of self-watering growing containers. Some alternatives include water-level indicators or viewing windows to see the water depth at the bottom of the container. Designs that enable a quick check of water level will reduce the guesswork involved when determining when to add more water to the growing containers.

POSSIBLE DRAWBACKS

The available space for crop growth is limited.

1 **3**

ADD THE HYDROPONIC SUBSTRATE AND PLANTS

1 Add the wicking rope to the self-watering growing container according to the manufacturer's instructions.

2 Fill the bottom 2 to 3 inches of the growing container net cup with prerinsed clay pellets. Clay pellets are often covered in dust, which is generally harmless, but the dust can unnecessarily create a mess in a new garden. This dust can easily be washed off the clay pellets with a quick rinse.

3 Fill the growing container with a hydroponic nutrient solution to a height just slightly above the clay pellets.

4 Place the stone wool blocks (with or without the already established seedlings) on top of the clay pellets, ensuring the bottoms of the blocks make contact with the nutrient solution. If you're using a new stone wool block without already established seedlings it is important to soak the new stone wool block in a hydroponic nutrient solution before adding to growing container.

5 Add prerinsed clay pellets around the stone wool blocks to secure them in place.

6 If you're using already established seedlings in the stone wool blocks skip to step 7. Otherwise add seeds to the stone wool blocks and cover them with clear plastic containers. The plastic containers should fit tightly around the blocks to trap humidity. After the seeds germinate, remove the clear plastic containers.

7 Lightly irrigate the top of the stone wool blocks with a nutrient solution twice per week for the first two weeks. This will help ensure the seedlings have enough time to develop roots that stretch downward into the nutrient solution at the bottoms of the growing containers.

8 After the transplants are established, continue to monitor water levels by either lifting the growing containers to see if they feel lightweight (no water) or use a water-level indicator buoy to determine the water level. Some growing containers have a clear window for viewing water level at the bottom of the growing container; this makes it much easier to quickly check water level instead of lifting up each growing container to see if it feels heavy or not.

THE NUTS AND BOLTS OF MAINTENANCE

IRRIGATION: Follow the Reservoir Management irrigation strategy detailed in section 4 on page 164.

PLANTING: Start seedlings in the stone wool blocks in separate systems or use clear plastic cups as humidity domes to start seedlings directly in the Corner Shelf garden.

SUITABLE CROPS: Use short-growing crops (max canopy height 6 inches) that tolerate light levels in the range of 200–350 umol/m2/s with a low root zone oxygen requirement.

IMPORTANT DETAILS

➡ For longer term crops such as the parsley and kale shown, which are capable of growing for several months or more if properly maintained, it is important to fully refresh the nutrient solution every month by dumping out any nutrient solution in the growing container and refilling it with a fresh mix. Plants uptake nutrients at different rates and over time this leads to deficiencies and toxicities of specific nutrients. It is important to reset the nutrient solution every month with long-term crops to minimize the risks of plants showing a response to nutrient deficiencies or toxicities.

➡ When harvesting, try to hold the crop over the edge of the container and then cut to minimize the amounts of loose debris falling into the growing container during harvest. Loose organic matter (leaves, stems, flowers, and so on) will rot in the growing container and attract pathogens and/or pests.

Bok choy, tatsoi, cabbage, cilantro, parsley, salad burnet, kale, Swiss chard, and mustard greens being harvested from the Corner Shelf garden.

BUILD DIFFICULTY	PRICE	ELECTRICAL REQUIREMENT	MAINTENANCE REQUIRED	PEOPLE REQUIRED	LIGHT INTENSITY
Moderate to High	High	116 W	Low to Moderate	1 to 2; requires lifting 50+ pounds	150–200 umol/m2/s

LIFT TOP COFFEE TABLE

THE MOVING COMPONENTS OF THIS LIFT TOP COFFEE TABLE design and need for creative power-cord management make this system a moderate to highly difficult build. The hydroponic system in this design is deep water culture (DWC), which is generally low maintenance and beginner friendly. This specific deep water culture (DWC) design is best suited for cuttings, making it possible to purchase cut herbs such as mint or basil from a grocery store and plant them directly into this garden.

An important note about this garden is it may not be well suited for gardeners who have limited mobility. The position of the garden is on the floor under a table, not an easy location to access and maintain. Personally, I find the joy of having a garden under my coffee table in my living room balances the increased effort required to access and maintain the garden. Please consider this trade off before building a garden similar to the one described.

ITEM	QUANTITY	DIMENSIONS
TABLE		
Lift top coffee table	1	36¼ in L x 26¼ in W x 19¼ in H
SURFACE AND WALLS		
Raised edge silicone waterproof mat	1	32 in L x 24 in W x 1 in H
Blackboards, 3/16-inch thick	2	25¾ in L x 3/16 in W x 7⅞ in H
Blackboards, 3/16-inch thick	2	36 5/16 in L x 3/16 in W x 7⅞ in H
Magnets	76	⅘ in L x ⅘ in W x 5/64 in H
GROWING CONTAINER		
Straight wall containers with lids	2	24 in L x 15 in W x 5 in H
Foam plugs	48	1 in L x 1 in W x 1 in H
Hydroponic fertilizer	1 lb	
ELECTRICAL COMPONENTS		
LED grow light bars, 10 W	4	24 in L x 1 in W x 1 in H
LED grow light bars power cords	2	
LED grow light bars connecting cords	3	
LED grow light square, 75 W, with hanging kit	1	9 15/16 in L x 9 15/16 in W x 1⅕ in H
Power strip with minimum two USB ports and three outlets	1	Minimum 5-foot cord length
Extension cord	1	Determine the length necessary to connect the table to the closest accessible outlet.
USB air pump, 5 V	1	
¼-inch air tube	1	4 ft
¼-inch barb tee	1	
Small air stones	2	
USB fans, dual 50 mm	2	11 15/16 in L x 1 15/16 in W x 25/32 in H
Cable clips, self-adhesive	20	1 3/16 in L x 13/32 in W x 9/32 in H
#6 ¾ inch screws	4	
Metal twist ties	4	

PAINTING MATERIALS

	QUANTITY	DIMENSIONS
Foodsurface-approved tabletop epoxy	1	2-quart kit
Chalkboard spray paint	1	
Disposable paintbrush	1	
Disposable mixing container	1	
Paint mixing stick	1	

TOOLS

Drill	Deburring tool	Marker	Scissors
⅞-inch drill bit	Ruler	Wood saw	Safety goggles

MATERIALS

Please read through the build guide before purchasing materials.

PREPARATION

1 Prepare the table for garden installation. If this is a new table, build it according to the manufacturer's manual. Position the table in its final location; it will be difficult to move after the system is installed.

2 If your table has dimensions different from the model used in this guide it is important to take the following measurements before ordering materials:

> ➔ Measure the available floor space under the table to select an appropriately sized silicone mat for leak protection.

A waterproof floor mat is a worthwhile addition to this system to contain drips, small leaks, or spills. It is difficult to remove the growing containers when they are full of water, a floor mat reduces the urgency to remove the growing containers to clean up small drips or spills that may occur when filling the reservoir or working with plants. Purchase the floor mat before the growing containers to get a true measurement of the space available after the mat is installed.

TABLE SELECTION

The most important decision in this garden is the table selection. This table was selected because when the top is lifted it exposes the floor underneath, providing access to the garden from above in addition to the removable side panels. There are many lift top tables and this hydroponic garden design can be modified to fit most of them, but it is important to consider how to access the garden and the amount of space the plants will have to grow both vertically and horizontally.

This design has many devices plugging into one power strip. It is important to consider how to position these devices to permit access to the power strip and minimize visibility of the power cords. It is also important to consider the maximum power capacity of the power strip and wall outlet. The power strip used in this design has a total capacity of 1250 W; all of the electrical components in this design, including LED bars, LED square, air pump, and fans, use a total of 116 W.

➔ Measure the inner dimensions of the silicone mat to select growing containers with the appropriately sized outer dimensions. Measure the available vertical space under the table to ensure there is at least 6 inches of clearance from the growing container surface to the grow lights. Remember to include the height of the grow lights when you're calculating the vertical space available for plants. This garden has 12³⁄₁₆ inches of vertical space under the table. The growing containers are 5 inches tall and the grow lights are 1 inch tall, leaving 6³⁄₁₆ inches clearance between the growing container surface and the grow lights.

➔ Measure the available space on the bottom of the table for mounting grow lights. Be aware that the power cord for the lights may add 1 to 3 inches to the overall length of the light. Consider the sizes of the growing containers as well when selecting lights. Lights smaller than the growing area may leave growing space underutilized while lights larger than the growing area will underutilize the output of the grow lights.

Leave an air gap between the light and the tabletop to allow heat to dissipate off the back of the light.

INSTALLING THE LIGHTS

1 Before installing the power strip or lights consider how to position these components to permit access to the power strip and minimize visibility of power cords. I highly recommend laying out all of the electrical components near their final locations to visualize how the power cords can be mounted or hidden to improve the overall aesthetics of the garden. Installing grow lights on the bottom of a table requires squeezing into tight spaces. I prefer to install lights before any of the other components to maximize the amount of workspace. Another option is to turn the table on its side during the light installation to avoid working on your back.

2 Install the 75 W LED square to the bottom of the lift top table before installing the LED bars along the perimeter. Many square LED lights come with a mounting kit. The mounting kit on this specific 75 W LED square, unfortunately, places the grow light very close to the growing surface (closer than 6 inches). Fortunately this LED square has four holes that perfectly fit the screws, enabling me to mount it directly to the tabletop. Be very careful when mounting to avoid screwing too deeply and breaking the surface of the tabletop! To avoid overheating the grow light or damaging the tabletop with heat from the light, leave an air gap between the light and the tabletop. This design uses four #6 2-inch screws to mount the LED square to the tabletop, leaving a ¾-inch air gap.

3 Loosely connect the 75 W LED square power cord to the lift top arms. After attaching the cord to the structure, carefully test lifting and lowering the tabletop while observing the cords underneath (this is best treated as a two-person job). Be mindful of any opportunities for the cable to be crushed, ripped, stretched, or damaged in any way by the moving table components.

4 Connect the power cords and daisy-chain connectors to the LED bars before installing them. The power cords add a couple inches to the length of the lights so it is important to test the lights to determine if they will fit with the cords connected before installing. All four of the 10 W LED bars in this design can be daisy chained together to use only one power cord, but this means all but one of the LED bars has cords connected to both ends (power in and power out). Unfortunately the light bars running along the width of the table do not fit when there is a cord connected to both ends. This garden instead connects power cords to each of the LED bars running along the length of the table and then those daisy chain to power a LED bar running along the width. Another option is to connect a dedicated power cord to each LED bar, but each additional power cord requires an outlet on the power strip and the cord needs space to mount discreetly to the bottom of the table. To minimize power cords, I recommended daisy-chaining LED bars as much as possible. Check the LED bar installation manual or contact the light manufacturer to find information on the maximum number of bars that can be daisy chained together safely.

This design uses self-adhesive cable clips to discreetly manage power cords on the bottom of the table. Another option for cable management is to use power cord raceway covers.

5 Mount the 10 W LED bars around the perimeter of the table. Most LED bars have mounting kits that may include brackets, zip ties, or double-sided adhesive stickers. The adhesive stickers mount the bars furthest from the growing surface to maximize the vertical growing space. Use double-sided adhesive stickers if available; otherwise, use whatever option places the grow lights the highest above the growing surface. The 10 W LED bars generate less heat than the more powerful 75 W LED square so leaving an air gap between them and the bottom of the table is not necessary.

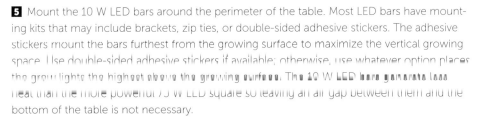

Attaching lights to a moving lift top creates a unique power-cord management challenge. The power cord for the LED square mounted to the bottom of the lift top is loosely attached to one of the arms holding up the tabletop surface. Carefully test opening and closing the lift top to ensure the power cord will not be crushed, stretched, or damaged in any way!

LIGHT SELECTION

Two different LED grow lights are used in this garden, which provide an average light intensity of 150–200 umol/m2/s PPFD. This is sufficient for most leafy greens and herbs but it is lower than reccomended for most flowering crops such as tomatoes and peppers. It may be possible to add additional light, but it is important to consider the amount of heat produced by grow lights; even this current design will generate a noticeable amount of heat. Reducing the light in this system is also possible but this will significantly reduce the number of crop options. If your table is smaller or you decide to allocate less of the space to growing, it may be possible to achieve a light intensity sufficient for most leafy greens while using only one of the lighting options detailed in this build guide. This garden has one LED grow light square and four LED grow light bars. The 75 W LED square is capable of delivering much higher light levels than the 10 W LED bars. At a distance of 6 inches from the light it delivers 350+ umol/m2/s and at 1 inch it delivers 150+ umol/m2/s. The drawback with the LED square is it struggles to evenly light over any growing area larger than 15 in L x 15 in W even when the light is placed 1 inch above the growing surface. At closer distances it struggles to evenly light any area larger than 12 in L x 12 in W. On the other hand, each 10 W LED bar lights up a large 24 in L x 6 in W section of the growing container surface but only delivers 100–130 umol/m2/s PPFD. It is much easier to evenly light a large growing area using multiple sources such as an array of LED bars instead of a single, more powerful source like the 75 W LED square in this design. This garden design positions LED bars close to the growing surface around the perimeter of the table and positions the more powerful LED square farther away from the surface by mounting it to the tabletop. By positioning low-intensity lights closer and high-intensity lights farther away from the growing surface, this design is able to deliver a relatively even light intensity to the entire growing area. It is important to note that the light intensity of all grow lights will diminish over time. Some grow lights experience a 10 to 20 percent reduction in output after one to three years.

BUILDING THE GROWING CONTAINERS

1 Mark the locations of plant sites with a ruler and marker. Use a dry erase marker if you do not plan on painting the container after drilling the holes. Along the length of the container there are six plant sites with the outer sites 3½ inches from the edge and 3 inches between sites. Along the width of the container there are four plant sites with the outer sites 3 inches from the edge and 2½ inches between sites. This garden has approximately twelve plant sites per square foot. Recommended plant spacings for popular hydroponic crops can be found in the Crop Selection Charts in the appendix on page 177.

2 Drill ⅞-inch holes at the intersections of the rows and columns to fit the 1-inch-wide foam plugs.

3 Remove any plastic shavings remaining on the hole edges with a deburring tool. At this point the growing container is usable; the additional painting step is optional.

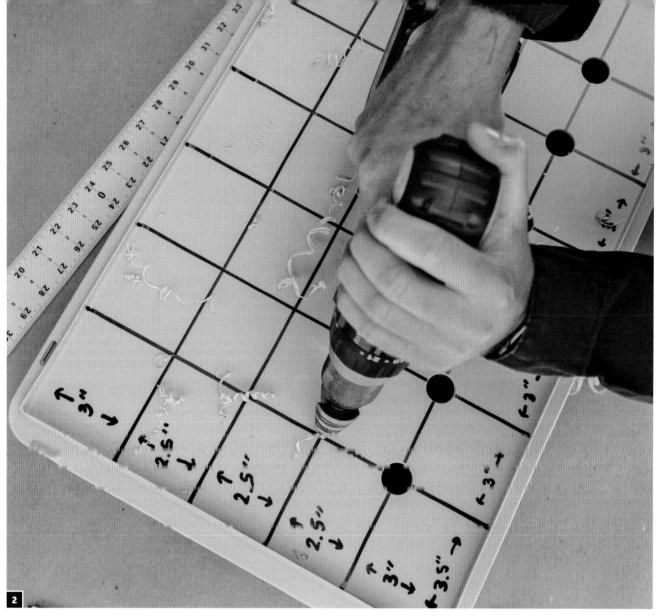

2

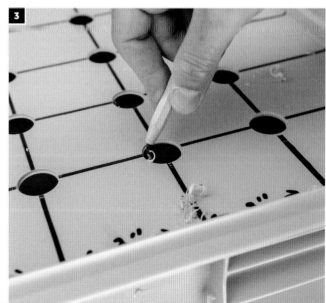

3

POSSIBLE DRAWBACKS

Installing lights under a coffee table can be challenging! This system does generate some noise, which can be distracting in a living room. The bright lights of the garden can also be distracting in a living room.

GROWING CONTAINER SELECTION

The available growing space under this table is 34¼ in L x 24¼ in W. To make this garden easier to clean, I decided to use two smaller growing containers instead of one large container. These two containers do not completely cover the space available under the table, which does reduce the yield potential of the system. This was a tradeoff with using prefabricated containers instead of building a container to cover the full growing space. If you'd like to maximize your garden space, you may be interested in building your own growing container similar to the one used in Stream of Greens described in section 3 on page 54. Be aware that it will likely be difficult to move a large growing container under a table and system cleaning will likely have to take place under the table. Smaller growing containers make it easier to remove the system for periodic cleanings. The containers in this design are 24 in L x 15 in W x 5 in H and require approximately 5¼ gallons (20 liters) of nutrient water to reach a water level ideal for cuttings. With this much water each container weighs nearly 45 pounds! A potential modification to this design could be the use of smaller containers. Replacing a large container with several smaller containers requires additional aeration equipment (tubing, air stones, and potentially another air pump), but this relatively small change could make a big difference when it comes to the long-term maintenance challenges of a hydroponic garden under a coffee table.

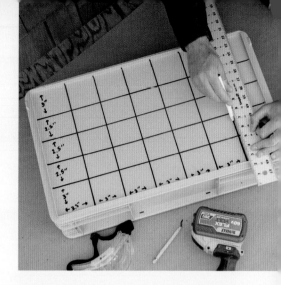

The containers I used in this design were the Uline Gray Straight Wall Containers 24 in L x 12 in W x 5 in H, but any straight wall container you can find will work as long as it fits the base. Unfortunately these containers were not available in black to match the base walls and table legs so they were painted black and coated in a tabletop epoxy resin approved for food-contact surfaces. Finding a properly sized container that is already a suitable color saves a lot of time!

OPTIONAL PAINTING

1 Flip over the lids of the growing containers and cover the plant site holes with painter's tape. Covering the bottoms of the holes will help keep the inside of the growing container clean during the painting and epoxy applications.

2 To avoid paint streaks on the sides of the container it is best to apply multiple light applications of spray paint. Wait a few minutes between applications to let the paint dry. These growing containers are painted with a chalkboard spray paint to match the chalkboard base walls.

3 After the spray paint fully dries the growing container surfaces can be coated with a layer of food-contact-approved tabletop epoxy. It is important to keep the painter's tape attached to the bottom of the lid for this step. Mix the two-part epoxy and apply a thick coat to the surface of the growing containers. I used approximately 6 ounces of epoxy to coat the lids of both containers.

4 The epoxy curing time will vary based on local conditions (i.e., temperature, humidity, light). Once the epoxy is fully cured, remove the painter's tape from the bottoms of the lids. Any epoxy covering the plant sites should easily peel away. Use the deburring tool to remove any stubborn epoxy pieces that do not peel away with the painter's tape.

BUILDING THE BASE WALLS

1 Cut two 25¾ in L x 7¹⁵⁄₁₆ in W sections of ³⁄₁₆-inch thick blackboard for the sides of the table.

2 Attach adhesive-backed magnets along the sides of the walls. Also attach a few adhesive-backed magnets along the bottom edges of the walls.

3 Using the magnets along the sides and bottoms, attach the two 25¾ in L x 7¹⁵⁄₁₆ in W wall sections to the table. It is important to attach the side walls before cutting the front and back sections to ensure the length of the front and back sections cover the exposed edges of the blackboard material.

4 Measure the length required to cover the front and back sections of the base including the exposed edges of the blackboard material used on the side walls. Without the side walls attached the front and back of this table measure 35¹³⁄₁₆ inches wide, but with the side wall additions they measure 36⁵⁄₁₆ inches.

5 Cut two 36⁵⁄₁₆ in L x 7¹⁵⁄₁₆ in W sections of ³⁄₁₆-inch thick blackboard for the front and back of the table.

6 Attach adhesive-backed magnets along the sides and bottom edges of the two 36⁵⁄₁₆ in L x 7¹⁵⁄₁₆ in W blackboard segments.

7 Add the front and back walls to the base of the table to ensure they fit well.

8 Remove all of the base walls and lightly spray paint them with multiple coats of chalkboard-colored spray paint.

An air pump and fans are not essential, but they will improve plant health. There are many air pump options, but for a living room coffee table with minimal free space, I prefer an air pump that is small and quiet. The small 5 V USB air pump used in this design is not powerful but it is very quiet. The small 5 V USB fans used in this design are also not powerful, but they are very quiet. An indication of adequate airflow is the visible movement of leaves. The two small fans in this design are capable of creating visible leaf movement while generating very little sound.

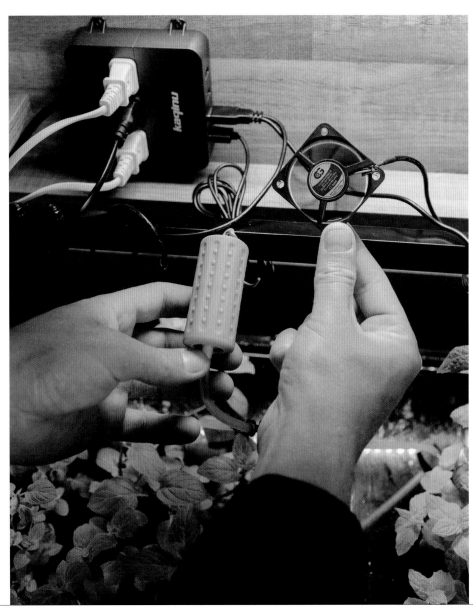

The air tube can enter the growing container through an existing plant site or through a hole created specifically for the air tube. An air tube hole should not be much larger than ¼ inch. An excessively large hole may allow light to enter the growing container, which potentially encourages algae growth. The foam used for holding cuttings in this design also works great for holding air tubes in place while blocking light from entering the growing container.

IMPORTANT DETAILS

➡ When selecting light bars, consider the additional leng,th of the light when they're connected to a power cord. The power cord may add an additional 1 to 2 inches to the length of the light. A 24-inch light may not fit in a 25-inch space after connecting the power cord!

➡ If possible, install the water-proof floor mat before purchasing growing containers. Measure the actual inner dimensions of the installed mat and then purchase growing containers with acceptable exterior dimensions.

➡ Do not rush to cut the front and back base walls! Position the side walls with attached magnets (or other fasteners) and measure the new length required to cover the front and back including the exposed edges of side walls.

INSTALLING AIR PUMP AND FANS

The target flow rate for an air pump depends on the crop selection, reservoir size, water temperature, and crop age. For most situations I target a flow rate of 1 L/min per 5 gallons, but lower flow rates can still provide a lot of benefit. For reference, the air pump used in the Lift Top Coffee Table design has an output of 0.24 L/min and the reservoir is a little larger than 5 gallons. A more powerful air pump might provide some benefit to the crop, depending on the crop selection, but that more powerful air pump would likely generate more noise.

1 Before attaching the ¼-inch air tube to the air pump, decide where you want to place the air pump. In this design the air pump has a metal hook and hangs from a metal cross-beam on the lift top table.

2 Measure the distance from the bottom of the air pump to the surface of the growing containers. Use this measurement to cut a segment of the ¼-inch air tube.

3 Attach the cut air tube segment to the middle barb on the ¼-inch barb tee.

4 Cut two 1½-foot segments of ¼-inch air tubes and attach them to the remaining two barbs on the ¼-inch barb tee.

THE NUTS AND BOLTS OF MAINTENANCE

IRRIGATION: Follow the Reservoir Management irrigation strategy detailed in section 4 on page 164.

PLANTING: Use cuttings or modify plant site hole size to fit net cups. Start plants directly in the garden or transplant seedlings from a separate system.

SUITABLE CROPS: Use short-growing crops (max height 6 inches along edges, 8 inches in the center) that can tolerate light levels in the range of 100–200 umol/m2/s with low to medium root zone oxygen requirements.

SOIL-BASED OPTION: Remove the growing containers completely and use the waterproof floor mat as a surface for traditional soil-filled garden pots.

Replacing the foam plugs with net cups enables this garden to grow a wide range of crops started from seed such as dwarf tomatoes and short-growing flowers. For examples of how to use net cups in a hydroponic garden see the Bar Tower, Lettuce Locker, or Salad Bowl garden designs in section 3.

5 Attach the air stones to the end of each 1½-foot air tube segment.

6 Connect the shorter segment of air tube from step 2 to the air pump.

7 The air stones should be positioned close to the middle of the inside of the growing containers to evenly aerate the reservoirs. The air tube with air stone can enter the reservoir through one of the plant site holes.

8 The fans can be positioned along the surface of the growing containers to push air through the lower canopy of the plants or they can be attached to the metal frame of the table using the same magnets used to attach the walls to the table legs.

The reusable foam plugs in this garden make it easy to plant cuttings from herbs such as mint and basil.

BUILD DIFFICULTY
High

PRICE
Moderate

ELECTRICAL REQUIREMENT
9 W

MAINTENANCE REQUIRED
Low to Moderate

PEOPLE REQUIRED
1

LIGHT INTENSITY
125–175 umol/m2/s

END TABLE

THIS GARDEN IS SMALL and will not yield a significant amount of edible produce, but what it lacks in functionality as a food-producing garden it more than makes up for with beauty. I try not to pick favorites among my many gardens but visitors to my home are quick to express their love for this garden. The process of building this garden covers almost every emotion: anticipation to build, excitement to select a wood block, surprise by the effort required to carve a wood block, fear the carving process will never end, relief when the carving process does end, happiness when you're able to add plants, and pride when seeing your completed hand-carved End Table garden.

ITEM	QUANTITY	DIMENSIONS
STRUCTURE		
Live edge redwood block	1	12 in L x 10 in W (Top) 8½ in L x 10 in W (Bottom) 6 in H
Tongue-and-groove redwood board, ¾ inch thick, with ¼ in W x ¼ in D groove centered along the ¾-inch-thick edge	1	Minimum board size: 27 in L x 1 in W x ¾ in H Actual board sized used: 48 in L x 5 in W x ¾ in H
Clear acrylic tabletop	1	12 in L x 10 in W x ³⁄₃₂ in H (~2.4 mm thick)
Heavy-duty hairpin legs with protector feet	4	16 in H
Oil wood finish	350 ml	
Adhesive door knob bumper pads, small clear rubber foot	8	1¹⁄₁₆ in x ¹³⁄₃₂ in H
#6 x 1¼-inch stainless steel screws	21	
1-inch tube straps	2	
Super glue for wood	1	
T50 ⅜-inch stainless steel staples	1–2 strips	
GROWING CONTAINER		
Plastic food-storage container, polypropylene (PP), ¾ oz	1	6⅞ in L 3⅞ in W x 2½ in H
Coco-cap, 6 inch	2	6⅖ in L x 6⅖ in W x 1⅘ in H
Hydroponic fill/drain combo kit	1	
2-inch net cup	1	
40 mm ping-pong ball, black	1	1⁹⁄₁₆ in (40 mm) diameter
GROW LIGHT		
LED grow light, 9 W	1	
12-foot 360 W socket gear switch for bulb lamp	1	12 ft power cord
Smart Wi-Fi single outlet	1	
SUBSTRATE		
Expanded clay pebbles	10 L	
OPTIONAL		
6½-inch brushed nickel perforated metal neckless lampshade	1	
1½-inch PVC pipe for supporting lampshade	1	3⅞ in length, outside diameter 1⁹⁄₁₀ in; inside diameter 1⅝ in

TOOLS

Drill	1-inch drill bit	Paintbrush	Step drill bit up to 1⅜-inch	Jigsaw (optional)
Sander (belt and/or orbital) with 80 and 150 grit	Die grinder	Wood chisel set (½ inch, ¾ inch, 1 inch)	16-ounce rubber mallet	Sandpaper sheets 60 and 150 Grit
Die grinder rotary burr bit set	Wood clamps	Staple gun	Hot glue gun (optional)	Scissors

The redwood block and board used to build this table were purchased from a local retailer that sells reclaimed and salvaged wood products that would otherwise be destined for a landfill. The tongue-and-groove redwood board is from an 1860s grain silo built on a farm in Half Moon Bay, California. The redwood block is from a fallen redwood tree collected only a few miles from my home. It may be difficult (or impossible) to find these specific materials, but it is not impossible to find or create similar blocks and boards from salvaged or harvested wood products in your area. Using refurbished wood adds character to a piece of furniture and can potentially lower the materials cost.

CARVING THE BLOCK

1 Check the block surfaces to see where they may need to be sanded to ensure a level top and bottom.

2 Secure the block to a stable and flat surface with wood clamps. Sand all sides of the block using first the 80 grit until surfaces are level, and then use the 150 grit to smooth the surface. The specific block used in this garden was very uneven, so I used a belt sander to remove wood until the block was level. Then I then switched to an orbital sander to smooth the surfaces. A belt sander can quickly remove a lot of wood from a surface and should be used with caution! The degree of sanding used on the live edges is a personal decision. I very lightly sanded the live edges with the orbital sander using a 150 grit. It is a difficult balance to maintain as much character on the block as possible while also creating a smooth, clean surface.

3 There are many ways to carve the block and while the following process may be laughed at by professional carpenters, I'm still happy with the final result. The rough shape of the interior of the block was chiseled using a wood chisel set and rubber mallet. This process is very time intensive! Early in the process it is easy to accidentally chip away pieces that run all the way to the edge of the block, so it is important to chisel out small sections at first to create the general hole shape.

3 **4**

4 Use a die grinder with a rotary burr bit set to finalize the shape of the carved-out section and smooth the surfaces. The die grinder with a burr bit is capable of removing a significant amount of wood and it can be used earlier in the carving process, replacing some of the chiseling work. However, I found the chisel is better for removing larger sections of wood and the die grinder for expanding the hole size by removing wood from the interior walls of the chiselled out hole.

5 Test fit the plastic food container into the carved-out hole. Expand the hole as necessary until container fits at the bottom and there is as much vertical space above the container as possible while maintaining a minimum of 1 inch of solid block between bottom of carved out hole and the bottom of block. The specific dimensions of the carved out section in this block are 9 in L x 8 in W at the top, 7 in L x 4 in W at the base, and 4½ inches deep.

6 Drill a 1-inch-diameter hole at the center of carved out section. This will be used for a drainpipe.

5

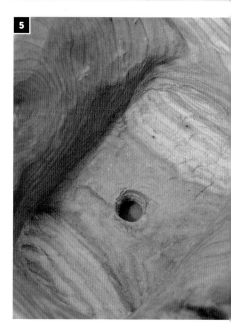

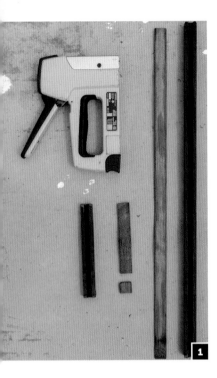

BUILDING THE LIGHT SUPPORT

There are many alternative ways to mount the grow light. One option that may be easier to assemble is to replace the wood support with 1-inch copper tubing and 90-degree elbows. With this method it may be necessary to disassemble the lamp cord to fit the cord through the tubing, but this still may be an easier option than building it out of wood. Another option is to still use wood or copper tubing but do not conceal the lamp cord inside. Many modern industrial style lampstands have exposed power cords so there may be both style and build difficulty factors to consider when deciding to conceal the lamp cord. Below is a guide for the light support with a concealed lamp cord within a salvaged tongue-and-groove redwood board.

1 Cut the ¾-inch-thick redwood board into the following segments:

→ 21 in L x ¾ in W x ⅝ in H, with ¼ in W x ¼ in D groove along 21 in L centered on ¾ in W

→ 6 in L x ¾ in W x ⅜ in H, with ¼ in W x ¼ in D groove along 6 in L centered on ¾ in W

→ 21 in L x ¾ in W x ⅛ in H

→ 4½ in L x ¾ in W x ¼ in H

→ ¾ in L x ¾ in W x ¼ in H

2 Attach the ¾ in L x ¾ in W x ¼ in H segment to the end of the 6 in L x ¾ in W x ⅜ in H segment so the smaller segment overhangs on the grooved side of the shorter segment. I've built this garden multiple ways using both staples and/or glue to assemble light stand. It is difficult to staple small segments without breaking them, so I recommend gluing the small segment instead of stapling it.

3 Position the socket end of the lamp cord at the small segment attached to 6-inch-long redwood segment.

4 With the lamp cord positioned in the groove of the 6-inch segment, position the 4½ in L x ¾ in W x ¼ in H segment over the cord and groove, leaving approximately ¾ inch of the groove exposed towards the end of the 6-inch segment opposite the bulb socket.

It is a good idea to line up the pieces before stapling or gluing to make sure there is enough room at the end of the 6-inch segment for the upright support without it overlapping the 4½-inch-long segment.

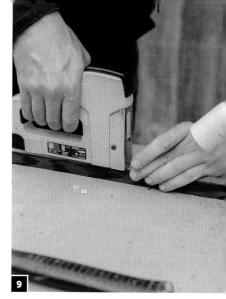

5 Attach the 4½-inch-long segment to the 6-inch-long segment using a staple gun or glue. The staples used in this build are 13⁄32 inch wide (10 mm), which is wide enough to avoid the groove and lamp cord (¼ inch or 6.35 mm) if perfectly positioned. In general I advise using glue to avoid the risk of stapling the lamp cord, which could be very dangerous.

6 Line up the 6-inch-long segment to the end of the 21-inch-long segment with the groove facing toward the lamp socket. Be sure to position the lamp cord down through the 21-inch-long segment groove. Holding these segments together, drill a pilot hole ⅛ inch from the end of the 6-inch segment straight down into the 21-inch segment.

7 Slowly screw in a 1¼-inch-long screw into the pilot hole made in step 6 to connect the 6-inch segment to the 21-inch segment.

8 Tuck the power cord into the groove on the 21-inch-long segment and cover with the 21 in L x ¾ in W x ⅛ in H segment.

9 Staple or glue the 21 in L x ¾ in W x ⅛ in H segment to the 21 in L x ¾ in W x ⅝ in H one. If you're stapling, be very careful not to staple through the power cord!

POSSIBLE DRAWBACKS

Carving the wood block is time intensive and getting the correct shape is challenging. The size of the growing container is fairly small in this garden and it may require multiple checks per week to ensure plants still have access to water.

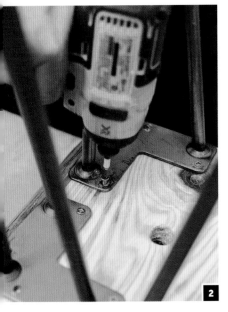

ASSEMBLE THE GARDEN

1 Position the hairpin legs on the bottom of the block.

2 Screw the legs to the bottom of the block.

3 Stand the block on its legs on a level surface.

4 Attach the light support to the block. Position the lamp support at the center of the longer side of the block. Hold it in place with a wood clamp. Use 1-inch tube straps to secure support to block. Do not overtighten the straps or you may damage the lamp support. Ensure the lamp support is upright using a vertical level before attaching the second tube strap. A later modification I made to this garden was to replace the galvanized steel tube straps with copper tube straps. There are many ways to make this garden your own with unique hardware, alternative wood species, or custom-made support legs!

5 Apply wood-conditioning oil according to instructions provided by manufacturer. Ensure the surface is clean before applying. On this design I applied the oil finish to all exposed wood except the bottom and live edge sides of the block. On other live edge wood projects, I have applied an oil finish to the live edge sides but in those cases I sanded the live edges much more than I did in this design. Applying wood-conditioning oil to the bottom of the block is optional based on personal preference. The manufacturer of this wood-conditioning oil says it is okay to fully coat all sides as the sealant is breathable. This means any moisture trapped in the wood can still escape even though the sealant is water-resistant, helping prevent any moisture from penetrating the wood. I have received recommendations from some woodworkers not to seal the bottom of a live edge slab to allow the wood to breath. I believe either method is acceptable and it's up to personal preference.

THE GROWING CONTAINER

There are many ways to modify the growing container in this design. It is possible to manage this garden without a drainage hole and simply add a rubber liner similar to the design seen in the Dinner Table design in section 3 on page 76. It is also possible to use self-watering containers such as those seen in the Corner Shelf garden in section 3 on page 98. I chose to build this growing container out of a small rectangular plastic food-storage container because I liked that it is low profile, removable, food safe, and inexpensive. Adding a drain to the growing container reduces the need for me to remove the growing container since it will be impossible to overwater and there is low risk of fertilizer buildup in the substrate since every few irrigations I can irrigate with just pure water. Gardens without drainage, such as the Dinner Table design in section 3 on page 76, will eventually need to be cleaned out as fertilizer buildup will eventually occur and certain nutrients will reach levels toxic to the plants.

1 Place the plastic food-storage container into the carved-out hole of the block.

2 Mark the location of the drain hole on the plastic food-storage container by inserting a marker through the bottom hole in the wood block.

3 Cut a 1⅜-inch-diameter hole in the plastic food-storage container at the marked location using a step drill bit.

4 Attach a drain fitting. This drain fitting was built for an Active Aqua Fill Drain Plumbing Kit, which includes a rubber gasket on both the fill and drain connections. Remove the rubber gasket from the drain connection and add it to the fill connection to create a seal with rubber gaskets on both the interior and exterior of the plastic food-storage container.

5 Add small clear rubber feet to each corner of the plastic food-storage container.

6 Return the plastic food-storage container to the carved-out hole in the block to check that it fits.

IMPORTANT DETAILS

This garden prioritizes aesthetics over plant happiness so it is important to select robust crops that can tolerate challenging growing conditions. Removing the clear tabletop, if you choose to use one, can significantly improve the growing conditions by improving airflow and increasing vertical growing space, but this does sacrifice some of the functionality of the end table.

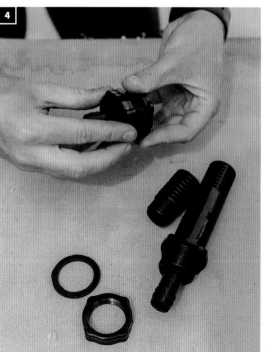

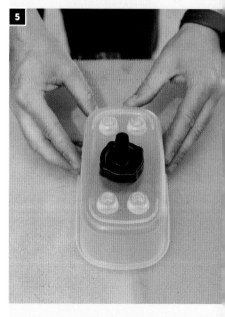

7 Remove the growing container from the block and test the seal of the drain fitting. Fill the growing container with water and check for leaks. Water should only be leaving the growing container through the ½-inch plastic pipe coming out from the bottom of the fitting. It is very important to test the seal of the growing container before adding plants.

8 A great way to beautify the food-storage growing container is adding a skirt to the rim to conceal the plastic container when positioned in the wood block. The skirt in this design is made from GROW!T Coco-Caps glued to the plastic rim of the plastic food-storage container but another option is to use burlap fabric. Other options for concealing the plastic growing container are to paint the container or simply allow the plants to grow large enough that they hide the plastic growing container.

9 There are many optional additions to the growing container to monitor moisture levels. Depending on the substrate used in the garden it may be possible to use a digital moisture sensor. A less expensive low-tech option used in this garden is a 2-inch-wide net cup and ping-pong ball similar to the Windowsill Herb Garden design in section 4 on page 66. When there is water in the bottom of the growing container, the ping-pong ball will float; simply tapping on the ping-pong ball can enable you to check the water level.

ADD HYDROPONIC SUBSTRATE AND PLANTS

1 Remove the growing container from the wood block before transplanting. Place a cup under the flood fitting to keep the container flat while you're working with it.

2 The flood fitting in the growing container only drains water after it reaches a certain height. This creates a small reservoir of water at the bottom of the growing container. It is important to fill this bottom portion of the growing container with a fast-draining substrate such as rocks or expanded clay pellets to avoid plants sitting in stagnant water.

This clear tabletop is not necessary, but it does transform the garden from "simply a garden" into a functional piece of furniture. You can create the tabletop by attaching small rubber feet to the corners of an appropriately sized glass or acrylic panel. The rubber feet lift the table top above the wood surface to improve airflow to the crop.

3 This garden is compatible with plants started in coco coir, stone wool, polymer-based plugs, or even traditional potting mixes. If you're using plants started in a traditional potting mix, it is best to rinse off as much of the potting mix from the roots as possible and then position the plants so theirs roots make contact with the top of the expanded clay pellets. Add additional clay pellets on top of the roots to hold the plants in position.

4 After transplanting, thoroughly water the garden until the water draining from the garden is free from loose substrate. Once the water draining from the growing container is clean, switch to watering the growing container with a nutrient solution to give the plants an initial feeding. After the growing container stops dripping, return it to the wood block.

5 Whenever you're watering the garden, place a cup or bowl under the table to collect any excess irrigation water draining from the bottom of the wood block.

LAMPSHADE

1 Cut a 3⅞-inch-long segment of 1½-inch PVC pipe.

2 Insert the lamp socket through the top of the lampshade, and PVC pipe, and then screw in the grow light bulb.

3 The PVC pipe should support the lampshade at a height that reduces the amount of light leaking outside of the growing space.

The lampshade is supported by a 1½-inch-diameter PVC pipe positioned between the lamp and the lampshade.

THE NUTS AND BOLTS OF MAINTENANCE

IRRIGATION: Follow the Drain-to-Waste irrigation strategy in section 4 on page 165.

PLANTING: It is possible to start plants directly in this End Table design, but this garden can be a challenging environment for some crops as it can experience warm temperatures with minimal airflow. It is best to use strong transplants that can handle the challenging environment long enough to adapt to the End Table garden and establish strong root systems.

SUITABLE CROPS: Use law-growing crops with light requirements in the range of 100–200 umol/m2/s.

SOIL-BASED OPTION: Replace the hydroponic growing container with soil-based pots or position small soil-based pots in the growing container. Remove potted plants when watering and allow the pots to fully drain before returning them to the wood block.

BUILD DIFFICULTY	PRICE	ELECTRICAL REQUIREMENT	MAINTENANCE REQUIRED	PEOPLE REQUIRED	LIGHT INTENSITY
Moderate to High	High	105 W	Moderate	1	Seedlings: 250–350 umol/m2/s Mushrooms: 175–250 umol/m2/s

CABINET FARM

The Lettuce Locker (left) and Cabinet Farm (right) designs are shown here.

THE CABINET FARM AND UPCOMING LETTUCE LOCKER are closed environment gardens built within metal lockers, but the general design can be adjusted to work in a variety of closed environments such as pantries or armoires. Generally homes have climates comfortable for humans, which is also ideal for most hydroponic crops, but creating a closed environment garden creates a microclimate that can be drastically different from the general climate within the home. Grow lights produce heat and plants transpire (release moisture into air); this combo leads to a warm, humid microclimate. If the general climate of a home is cold and dry, a warmer, wetter microclimate is beneficial but if the climate within the home is already ideal for the selected crop, then a

ITEM	QUANTITY	DIMENSIONS
STRUCTURE		
Blue two-door metal cabinet	1	39²/₅ in W x 15⁴/₅ in D x 25¹/₁₀ in H
4-inch ceiling collars	2	
Magnetic tape roll, ½ in x 10 ft	1	
Electrical tape, ¾ in x 25 ft	1	
~~Aluminum foil a material~~	1	~~100 in L x 10 in W x 10 in H~~
1¼-inch-diameter magnetic hooks, max force 14 lb	3	
Exhaust fan bug shields, 4 to 6 inches	2	
Foil repair tape 1⅞ in x 30 ft	1	
Dryer vent cover, 4-inch	1	
#6-32 x ½-inch Philips flathead stainless steel machine screws	4	
#6-32 x 2-inch Philips flathead stainless steel machine screw	1	
#6-32 stainless steel machine screw nuts	4	
#6-32 stainless steel machine screw wing nut	1	
³/₁₆-inch x 1-inch metallic stainless steel fender washer	1	
ELECTRICAL COMPONENTS		
18 W LED strip light, 18 inches	2	18 in L
76 W LED strip light, 7 foot	1	7 ft L
Exhaust fan, 4 inches, 160 CFM, 18 W	1	
6-inch fan with clip attachment, 15 W	1	
Power strip, 15 amp/125-volt capacity	1	
Smart Wi-Fi single outlets	2	
Desktop CO2 monitor	1	
MUSHROOM KIT		
Mushroom grow kit, oyster		
Mushroom grow kit, pink oyster		

TOOLS

Drill	4½-inch hole saw, bimetal drill bit for thin metal	2-inch hole saw, bi-metal drill bit for thin metal	⁵/₃₂-inch drill bit
Marker	⁵/₁₆-inch wrench	Ruler	Safety goggles
Work gloves	Tape	Electrical Tape	

Horizontal shelves are a blank canvas for growing systems. This build guide uses the top shelf for mushrooms and the lower shelf for seedlings or herbs, but this layout could easily be modified to be all mushrooms, all plants, or any combination of the two.

closed environment garden will require dedicated climate control equipment to manage the heat and humidity. (Also see the Crop Selection Charts in the appendix on page 177 for target climates for popular hydroponic crops.) Climate control equipment greatly increases the cost of a home garden design and the equipment can potentially generate a lot of noise. I love growing in my Cabinet Farm and Lettuce Locker, especially in winter when my home is cold and dry, but the simple design choice to garden in a closed environment does increase the cost to build this garden as well as making it more challenging to maintain.

PREPARATION

1 Select a location with access to power outlets, preferably close enough to conceal exposed cords coming from the back of the Cabinet Farm.

2 Assemble the two-door metal locker according to instructions provided by the manufacturer. This build guide involves drilling a couple of holes in the exterior of the locker. Depending on your selected location for the garden, it may be best to assemble and drill through locker in an alternative location and then move the locker to its final location after completing the messy process of drilling through metal.

BUILDING THE STRUCTURE

1 Drill a 2-inch hole through the back of the locker for the power cords. I positioned this hole at the top left of the back, closest to the nearby power outlet. The best location for this hole will depend on the location of power outlets relative to the Cabinet Farm in your location. Always wear eye protection when drilling through metal!

2 Drill a 4½-inch hole through the side of the locker for the exhaust fan. The locker in this design has small vents located near the top of the doors so positioning the exhaust fan on the lower level encourages air to enter through these vents then flow over the mushrooms before moving to the lower level through a gap between the middle shelf and back wall of locker. This airflow design pulls in fresh air for mushrooms and directs the carbon dioxide-rich air from near the mushrooms to the carbon dioxide-hungry plants on the lower level. The precise location of the 4½-inch hole can be determined by placing the exhaust fan in the desired location and tracing the outline of the fan on the locker wall. Then mark the center of the traced outline as the drill location for the 4½-inch hole.

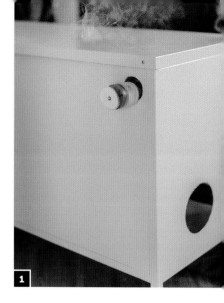

MUSHROOMS

A small mushroom grow kit can yield handfuls of mushrooms in one week! Watching mushrooms nearly double in size from morning to night is shocking, especially when they're grown side-by-side with plants that typically take months to mature. I admittedly have little experience growing mushrooms and still have a lot to learn, so this book has limited mushroom cultivation information. But based on my experience thus far, I've found it very easy to grow great-tasting mushrooms very quickly both with mushroom grow kits and inoculated logs. The mushroom logs take much larger (more than six months) to start producing harvestable mushrooms, but they require much less maintenance than the grow kit bags. I personally like how the logs look in the Cabinet Farm but the quick gratification of growing a huge mushroom crop in a week with a mushroom kit makes it very tempting to fill the entire garden with mushroom grow kits and forgo the old mushroom logs.

Small oyster mushrooms are shown emerging from a six-month-old inoculated log.

MUSHROOMS AND CARBON DIOXIDE

Growing mushrooms in the Cabinet Farm design can greatly increase the garden's overall productivity but the addition of mushrooms does create additional challenges when growing in a closed environment. Mushrooms release a lot of carbon dioxide, and while plants do take in carbon dioxide, the rate of carbon dioxide released greatly exceeds the rate of carbon dioxide taken in by the plants. Additionally mushrooms release carbon dioxide all day while most plants only take in carbon dioxide when exposed to light. High carbon dioxide levels can slow mushroom development and lead to elongated or deformed growth. On a kitchen counter, where there is natural airflow, it is possible to grow mushrooms without concern of high carbon dioxide levels inhibiting growth but in a closed environment such as the Cabinet Farm, the carbon dioxide levels can quickly spike to over 2000 ppm if you're not constantly running the exhaust fan. The recommended carbon dioxide levels for most oyster mushroom varieties are less than 800 ppm. Carbon dioxide monitoring equipment, as shown, can help gardeners determine exhaust fan set points including on-time frequency and fan speed.

GROWING PROCESS FOR MUSHROOM KITS

→ Cut open the bag and scrape the surface with a fork.

→ Submerge the mushroom bag in water for 6 to 10 hours.

→ Mist the surface and mushrooms daily

3 The exposed edges of newly drilled holes are very sharp. A layer of electrical tape on the exposed edges can help reduce the risk of cutting yourself or power cords on the sharp edges.

4 Position a 4-inch ceiling collar over the 4½-inch hole created for the exhaust fan. An additional 4-inch ceiling collar can also be positioned on the exterior of the locker if desired. Line the ceiling collar with magnetic tape to attach it firmly to the metal locker.

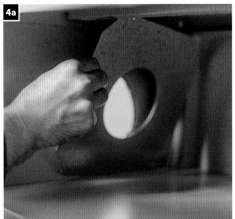

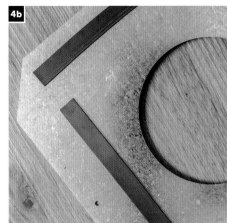

CREATING VENTILATION

This design has two fans, an exhaust fan on the lower level and a circulation fan on the top level. There are many ways to modify this design and it may be possible to grow healthy mushrooms and plants with just an exhaust fan, but the circulation fan helps ensure there are no areas of stagnant air in the locker. The specific circulation fan used in this design originally came with a clip-on attachment that I removed to bolt the fan directly to the metal shelf. There are many alternative fan options including most small desk fans as long as they fit within the height limitations of the shelf.

Generally, an insect screen is placed on the air intakes to prevent insects from entering the garden, but in this design the primary role of the insect screen is to capture spores released by the mushrooms. To maximize the efficiency of your exhaust fans regularly clean the insect screen or have replacements on hand.

POSSIBLE DRAWBACKS

The irrigation with this system is manual, which greatly simplifies the system reducing potential for mechanical errors, but it increases the potential for human error if plants are not checked frequently and irrigated as needed. Mushrooms grow fast and require daily misting. Spores released by mushrooms can dirty exhaust fan filter and those may need to be washed frequently.

INSTALLING THE GROW LIGHTS

This garden has three grow lights: two 18-inch lights for plants on the lower level and a single 3-foot light for the mushrooms on the top level. For simplicity I used three lights from the same manufacturer that can be linked together, but this delivered higher than necessary light levels to the mushrooms as mushrooms require very little light. There are many ways to modify the grow light layout in this garden including replacing the mushroom light with a low wattage strip light or greatly increasing the light levels by placing two 3-foot-long lights on each level to maximize the plant-growing potential of the garden! In this design the 3-foot light is mounted with magnetic hooks; this option could also be used to mount the 18-inch lights on the lower level, but this would potentially reduce the vertical growing space for the lower level plants.

1 Most grow lights include mounting hardware designed to be screwed into wood. Replace the included screws with #6 ½-inch flat tip stainless steel machine screws (bolts) and connect the mounts to the back of the two 18-inch grow lights.

2 The two 18-inch grow lights mount on the middle shelf to light the lower level. The lights are positioned parallel to each other at 3½ inches and 10½ inches from the front of the locker. Place the grow lights in the desired location and then mark the location of the machine screws on the middle shelf with a marker. Drill ⁵⁄₃₂-inch holes at each of the marked locations.

3 Secure the 18-inch grow lights to the middle shelf with #6 stainless steel machine screw nuts.

4 The 3-foot light on the top level of this garden is secured to the top of the locker with two magnetic hooks instead of machine screws. Machine screws and nuts are also an option for the top level, but I wanted to avoid creating holes in the top surface of the locker. Mount the 3-foot light near the front of the locker and direct the light toward the back of the locker by securing the lip of the light hood to the top of the locker with a heavy-duty block magnet.

5 Daisy chain the grow lights together with the included link cables and connect the cord to a smart Wi-Fi outlet to program on/off times for the lights.

Short-growing crops such as watercress work great in this garden. This crop of upland cress and chives is growing in a low-maintenance floating raft garden.

ADDING THE FINISHING TOUCHES

→ Plug in all electrical components to a power strip placed inside the Cabinet Farm or directly to an outlet outside of the locker.

→ Add plants! This garden is similar to the Bar Cart design in that both center their growing system around a 1020 tray. For more information on the many growing method options for 1020 trays, including floating raft hydroponics, see the Bar Cart garden in section 3 on page 60 or Propagation in section 4 on page 157.

→ Add a carbon dioxide monitor, hygrometer, and/or a thermometer to monitor the climate within the locker.

→ Adjust exhaust fan on-time and fan speed to modify the climate within the locker. Higher fan speeds and longer on-times can help reduce humidity, temperatures, and carbon dioxide levels. The primary drawback of setting the exhaust fan to a higher speed and longer on-time is the increased noise generated by the fan.

THE NUTS AND BOLTS OF MAINTENANCE

IRRIGATION: Follow the No Reservoir and No Leachate irrigation strategy detailed in section 4 on page 165.

PLANTING: Start seedlings directly in the garden or transplant seedlings started elsewhere.

SUITABLE CROPS: Use short-growing crops (max height 4 inches) that can tolerate light levels in the range of 250–350 umol/m2/s.

SOIL-BASED OPTION: Use traditional soil-filled pots and place them in the 1020 tray. Remove the pots when watering to allow them to drain elsewhere before returning them to the 1020 tray.

BUILD DIFFICULTY	PRICE	ELECTRICAL REQUIREMENT	MAINTENANCE REQUIRED	PEOPLE REQUIRED	LIGHT INTENSITY
High	High	111 W	Moderate	2	200–250 umol/m2/s at 12 inches, 300–400 umol/m2/s at 6 inches, 600–650 umol/m2/s at 4 inches

LETTUCE LOCKER

THE LETTUCE LOCKER is one of the more challenging garden designs detailed in this book. The wall of crops looks amazing but vertical tower gardens are often more difficult to operate and maintain. Besides looking cool, vertical tower gardens can pack a lot of crops into a small footprint while using less irrigation equipment compared to a multi-level horizontal system. Building the vertical towers can be relatively inexpensive; however, in this design the expense of the other materials, including the locker and grow lights, quickly adds up to land this design in the higher price range relative to other designs. The Lettuce Locker garden pairs perfectly with the Cabinet Farm design detailed earlier in this section. If you're building the Lettuce Locker as a standalone unit without the Cabinet Farm it will be necessary to modify the design to include an exhaust fan positioned preferably near the top of the locker. For more information on the exhaust fan please see the Cabinet Farm build guide.

ITEM	QUANTITY	DIMENSIONS
STRUCTURE		
Blue metal locker	1	15¹³⁄₁₆ in L x 14¹⁵⁄₁₆ in W x 72¹³⁄₁₆ in H
Wood box (used wine shipping box)	1	14 in L x 12 in W x 8³⁄₈ in H
Pond liner	1	4 ft L x 3 ft W
³⁄₈-inch stainless steel staples	50	½ in W x ³⁄₈ in H
4-in ceiling collar	2	
Magnetic tape roll, ½ inch x 10 feet	1	
1½-inch x 5-foot white furniture-grade schedule 40 PVC pipes	2	Outside diameter: 1¹⁵⁄₁₆ inches Inside diameter: 1⁵⁄₈ inches
1½-inch white furniture-grade PVC 45-degree elbows	2	
PVC water pipe clamps, 50 mm	2	Outer dimensions: 2⁹⁄₃₂ in L x ¹¹⁄₁₆ in W x 2¹⁄₁₆ in H Inner diameter: 2 inches
1½-inch plastic pipe caps	2	
Hydroponic net cup		Outer diameter at top: 1⁵⁄₁₆ inches Inner diameter at top: ¹³⁄₁₆ inch Outer diameter at bottom: ¹¹⁄₁₆ inch Height: 1³⁄₈ inches
Cord cover channel/raceway kit	1	Channels: 45 in L x 1½ in W x ¾ in D
1¼-inch-diameter magnetic hooks, max force 14 lb	2	
#6-32 x ½-inch Philips flathead stainless steel machine screws	2	
#6-32 stainless steel wing nuts	2	
⁷⁄₁₆ x 1 inch metallic stainless steel fender washers	2	
5 mm nickel-plated angled shelf supports	1	
Electrical tape, ¾ inch x 66 feet	1	
Double-sided mounting tape	1	1- x 400-inch roll
Rubberbands	2	
3½-inch pressed wool felt wicking mat fabric	1	10 ft L x 3½ in W
IRRIGATION		
½-inch black vinyl tubing	8 feet	
¼-inch black vinyl tubing	2 feet	
½-inch ball valves with barbed fittings	2	
¼-inch ball valves with barbed fittings	2	
¼-inch barbed connectors	2	
ELECTRICAL COMPONENTS		
48 W LED strip light, 4 feet	2	4 ft L
Smart Wi-Fi single outlet	1	
Hygrometer/thermometer combo	1	
6-inch fan with clip attachment, 15 W	1	
Submersible water pump, 400 GPH	1	

PAINTING MATERIALS

All-purpose white interior/exterior multisurface primer, sealer, and stain blocker	1 quart

TOOLS

Drill	4½-inch hole saw, bimetal drill bit for thin metal	2-inch hole saw, bimetal drill bit for thin metal	Step drill bit
Marker	Ruler	Staple gun	Drip irrigation cutter/hole punch tool
Wood clamps	Safety goggles	Work gloves	Scissors
PVC pipe cutter	Deburring tool		

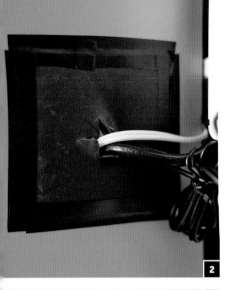

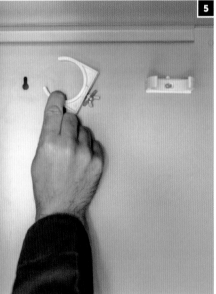

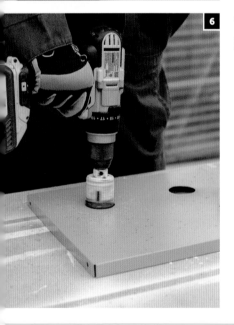

PREPARATION

1 Select a location with access to power outlets, preferably close to the Lettuce Locker to minimize the amount of exposed power cords.

2 Assemble the locker according to instructions provided by the manufacturer. This build guide involves drilling a couple holes in the exterior of the locker. Depending on the selected location for the garden it may be best to assemble and drill through the locker in an alternative location and then move the locker to its final location after completing the messy process of drilling through metal.

BUILDING THE STRUCTURE

1 Drill a 2-inch hole through the side of the locker for power cords. I positioned this hole midway on the right side of the locker close to a nearby power outlet. The best location for this hole will depend on the location of power outlets relative to the Lettuce Locker in your build. Always wear eye protection when drilling through metal!

2 Cover the sharp edges of the 2-inch hole with electrical tape and then cover the 2-inch hole with a 4 in W x 4 in L segment of pond liner. Tape the pond liner square into position with electrical tape. Cut a small X into the pond liner to create a passage for electrical cords that minimizes the amount of light and air escaping the locker.

3 Drill a 4½-inch hole for an exhaust fan. In this design the Lettuce Locker is paired with the Cabinet Farm and the location of the hole was selected based on the position of the exhaust fan in the Cabinet Farm. Another option is to add a shelf near the top of the locker to support an exhaust fan, which intakes hot air rising up past the towers and removes that air as exhaust through either the side or top of the locker.

4 Position a 4-inch ceiling collar over the 4½-inch hole created for the exhaust fan. An additional 4-inch ceiling collar can also be positioned on the exterior of the locker if desired. Line the ceiling collar with magnetic tape to attach it firmly to the metal locker. See the Cabinet Farm design for more information.

5 Install PVC water pipe clamps in the preexisting holes through the back of the locker using a ½-inch stainless steel machine screw, wing nut, and ³⁄₁₆- x 1-inch fender washer. The wing nut and washer are positioned on the back side of the locker.

6 Drill two 2-inch holes in one of the locker shelves. The centers of the drain holes are positioned 4¼ inches from the sides and 4¼ inches from the back.

CONSTRUCTING THE TOWERS

The towers in this garden are made from schedule 40 furniture-grade PVC pipe that does not contain heavy metals, noxious dioxins, or phthalates. This type of PVC pipe is slightly more difficult to work with as it is not as pliable as standard PVC pipe.

1 Cut two PVC pipes to 51½ inches using the PVC pipe cutters. Additionally, cut two 1 ½-inch-long PVC pipe segments.

2 Secure the PVC pipes to a worktable using wood clamps. Drill ⅞-inch holes for the plant sites using a step drill bit. The optimal spacing of the plant sites will depend on the selected crops (see the Crop Selection Charts on page 177 for recommended spacing for popular hydroponic crops). In this design the plant sites are spaced 6 inches apart with the first site positioned 7 inches from the top on one tower and 4 inches from the top on the other tower. The tower with the first site that's 7 inches from the top has 7 total sites and the other tower has 8 total sites.

3 Use the deburring tool to remove any PVC burrs on the plant site holes.

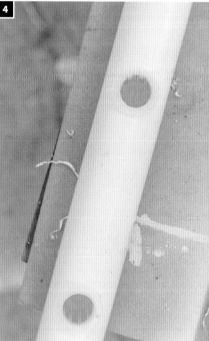

4 Test fit the net cups into the plant sites and use the deburring tool to expand the hole sizes if necessary. The net cups should fit snugly into the drilled plant sites. If the hole size is too large it is possible to wrap the net cups with plumber's tape to make them wider to create a tighter fit.

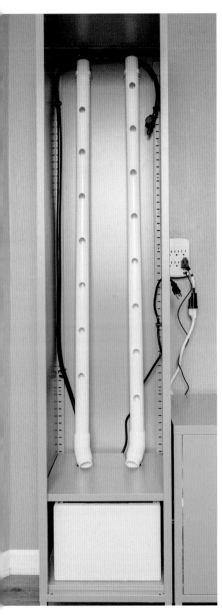

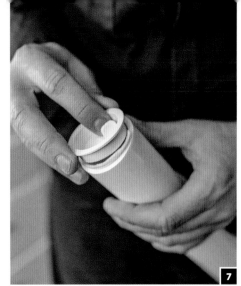

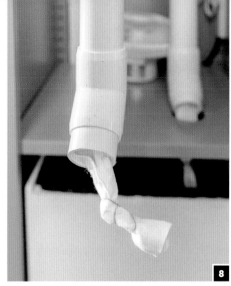

5 Drill a ⅜-inch hole in both of the 1½-inch pipe test caps with the step drill bit.

6 Cut two 5-foot-long segments of 3½-inch-wide pressed wool felt wicking mat fabric. Install the fabric along the back of the pipe opposite of the plant sites.

7 Use the 1½-inch pipe test caps to secure the fabric along the top rim of the PVC pipe towers.

8 Wrap the fabric extending from the bottom of the towers with a rubber band. This helps make the fabric more manageable when moving the towers and creates less exposed surface area to reduce potential algae development.

SETTING UP THE IRRIGATION MANIFOLD

1 Cut a 67-inch and a 19-inch segment of ½-inch black vinyl tubing.

2 Cut two 4¾-inch and two 1½-inch segments of ¼-inch black vinyl tubing.

3 Using the drip irrigation hole punch, create two holes in the 19-inch-long segment of ½-inch tubing. The holes in this design are positioned at 2½ inches and 3½ inches from the end of the ½-inch tube.

4 Insert ¼-inch barbed connectors into the holes punched in step 3.

5 Connect the 4¾-inch- and 1½-inch-long segments of ¼-inch black vinyl tubing with the ¼-inch ball valves.

6 Connect the 1½-inch-long segments of ¼-inch black vinyl to the ¼-inch barbed connectors from step 4.

7 Connect a ½-inch ball valve to both ends of the 19-inch-long segment of ½-inch tubing.

8 Connect the 67-inch- and 19-inch-long segments of ½-inch black vinyl tubing with a ½-inch ball valve. Orient the 19-inch-long segment so the ¼-inch emitters are close to the ball valve connecting the 67-inch- and 19-inch-long segments of ½-inch tubing.

9 Connect the 67-inch-long segment of ½-inch tubing to the submersible water pump.

The white reservoir at the base of the garden is made from a box that was originally used to transport wine bottles that I purchased from a liquor store. The reservoir holds a pump that pushes water up the side of the locker through a ½-inch black vinyl tube. Along the top of the locker two ¼-inch tubes connect to the ½-inch black vinyl tube to deliver water to each tower. To control flow rate there is a ½-inch ball valve on the ½-inch tube and ¼-inch ball valves on each of the ¼-inch tubes.

10 Build or find a reservoir with the following dimensions: 14 in L x 12 in W x 8⅜ in H. The reservoir in this design is made from a wood box originally used to ship wine. The box measures 14 in L x 12⅜ in W x 8⅜ in H, which is slightly wider than desired. The extra width of this specific reservoir still fits in the locker, but I was unable to add/remove the reservoir from the locker without disassembling the locker door (which is a minor inconvenience). The box was painted white with an all-purpose white interior/exterior primer, sealer, and stain blocker paint. After the paint dries, install the pond liner. See the Bar Tower design on page 66 for a detailed guide on installing a pond liner in a wood box.

11 Install the reservoir into the locker and then position the shelf with 2-inch drilled holes just above it. Add the pump to the reservoir and guide the ½-inch black vinyl tubing along the side of the locker. Bend the ½-inch tubing along the top of the locker to position the ¼-inch emitters near the top of the towers. The irrigation can be secured in place with cord cover channels and/or magnetic hooks.

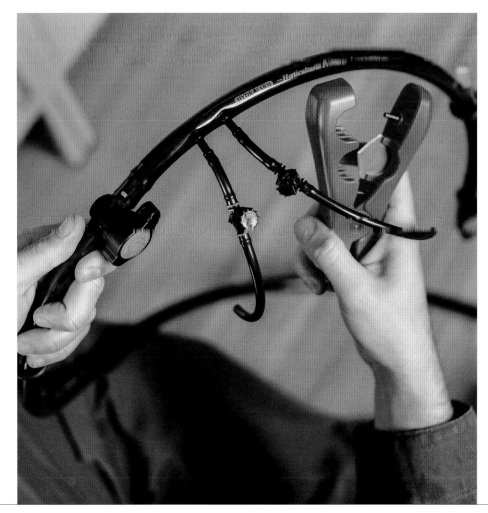

A drip irrigation hole punch makes it easy to create holes large enough to fit the ¼-inch barbed connectors yet not so large that there might be leaks at the connection.

POSSIBLE DRAWBACKS

This garden can get loud with the combined noise of a circulation fan, exhaust fan, and water pump. This garden functions best in homes with cool temperatures as heat released by the grow lights can build up in enclosed space even with exhaust fans. As with most vertical gardens, this garden is susceptible to leaks if the plugs are improperly placed. Plants in a skinny vertical tower often entangle their roots with neighboring plants, making it difficult to remove and replace individual plants without damaging others. System cleaning requires more disassembly work than most other hydroponic gardens. If the pump filter is not cleaned, emitters may clog and plants could dry out.

INSTALLING GROW LIGHTS

This garden has two 48 W 4-foot-long LED grow lights that provide more than enough light for most leafy greens crops. During the summer I had issues with heat buildup in the garden so I disconnected the daisy chain between the two lights to operate the garden using just one 48 W LED grow light. In the winter when there were fewer issues with heat buildup, I reconnected the daisy chain between the lights to operate the garden with two 48 W lights. If you know your selected location might experience temperatures over 75 degrees F and you want to grow crops that prefer cooler weather (such as lettuce), you may want to modify the lighting design by selecting lower wattage lights and/or using fewer lights.

1 Detach the locker door and move it to flat surface.

2 Attach the light mounts included with the strip lights to the 5 mm angled shelf supports.

3 Slide the shelf supports into the vents at the top of the locker door.

4 Attach the strip lights to the light mounts connected to the locker door. Arrange the lights so the power cord can connect to the top of the light closest to the door hinge. The light farther from the door hinge should be oriented to easily daisy chain the two lights together.

5 Attach the lower end of the strip lights to the locker door with double-sided mounting tape.

6 Connect the lights to a Smart Wi-fi outlet and program the on/off times to a photoperiod suitable for the selected crops. See the Crop Selection Charts on page 177 for recommended photoperiods for popular hydroponic crops.

7 If you wish, conceal the power cords with cord channels.

ADD-ONS

➡ Depending on the reservoir dimensions, it may be difficult to move the reservoir when adding additional nutrient solution. A funnel makes it easy to add water through the 2-inch drain holes in the locker shelf. This funnel is attached to a 3½ in L x ¾ in D black vinyl tube that drains into the reservoir.

➡ A water-level indicator makes it easy to quickly check if the reservoir needs additional water. This water-level indicator is ½-inch wide and pushed through a 3 ½ in L x ¾ in D black vinyl tube. The soft ¾-inch tube makes it possible to secure the water-level indicator in the available space in the 2-inch drain holes cut into the locker shelf. Another option is to create a dedicated hole in the locker shelf for a water level indicator.

➡ It may be possible to get adequate airflow in this garden with just an exhaust fan, but an additional small fan pushing air through the crop canopy helps remove pockets of hot humid air and strengthens plants. This fan is positioned to encourage an upward airflow to push heat up and out through the vent in the locker door.

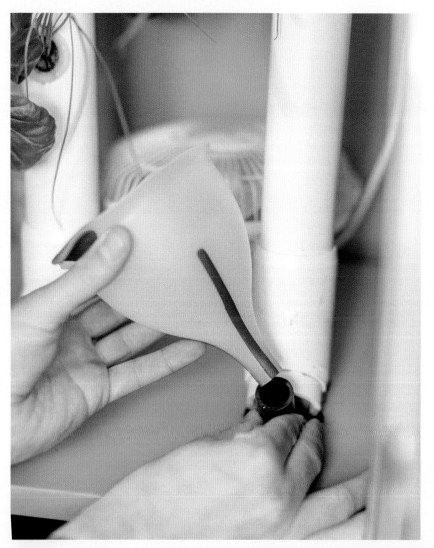

THE NUTS AND BOLTS OF MAINTENANCE

IRRIGATION: Follow the Reservoir Management irrigation strategy detailed in section 4 on page 164.

PLANTING: Transplant seedlings started in a separate system.

SUITABLE CROPS: Use short-growing crops that can tolerate light levels in the range of 200–650 umol/m2/s.

ADD PLANTS

This garden requires seedling transplants started in a plug appropriately sized for the net cups. The seedlings shown were grown in plugs that measure 25 mm wide (1 inch) and 40 mm tall (1⁹⁄₁₆ inches). The net cups in this design have an inner diameter of ¹³⁄₁₆ inch at the top and are 1⅜ inches tall. Cut away the lower halves of the net cups to allow the plugs to extend past what would be the bottoms of the net cups. It is necessary to squeeze the plugs to fit them into the net cups as the diameter of the plugs is larger than the diameter of the net cups. In a vertical tower garden, it is best to have tight-fitting plugs and net cups to limit the risk of leaks out the front of the tower. Push the seedlings deep into the net cups to ensure the bottom of the plug makes contact with the fabric mat along the back of the tower. If seedlings dry out in the first couple days try the following options:

➡ Pull out plug and check to see if fabric along the back of the tower is wet. If the fabric is not wet, it may be necessary to position the ¼-inch irrigation tube differently to ensure water is directed to the back of the tower.

➡ Push the seedlings deeper into the tower to ensure they have contact with the fabric.

➡ Cut small segments of the fabric and wrap the bottoms of seedlings to make them longer. The goal is to create a wicking strip directly to the plug to enable it to access water along the back of the tower while a plant matures to a size large enough to access that water directly with its roots.

**BUILD
DIFFICULTY**

Moderate

PRICE

Moderate

**ELECTRICAL
REQUIREMENT**

18 W unless
natural light is
available

**MAINTENANCE
REQUIRED**

Low to
Moderate

**PEOPLE
REQUIRED**

1

**LIGHT
INTENSITY**

Very low;
50–150
umol/m2/s

BATHROOM FLOWER GARDEN

THE BATHROOM IS A SURPRISINGLY GREAT LOCATION for hydroponic gardens as long as there is enough light, whether natural sunlight or supplemental light from a grow light. Bathrooms already have a water source and convenient drains for cleaning out a hydroponic garden. To avoid scaring dinner guests, you may not want to plant edible crops in your bathroom that are used to cook their dinner, but a garden can provide so much more than food. The purpose of this bathroom garden is to look and smell great. A mix of flower bulbs and scented herbs can pack a bathroom with attractive aromas that may turn the bathroom into your new favorite room. With the addition of some colorful houseplants this garden can be both attractive and aromatic. The biggest challenge with this garden is providing sufficient light. My bathroom has a window above the toilet that provides just enough light for flower bulbs and some houseplants, but if your bathroom does not have natural light it will be necessary to add a grow light. Even gardens in bathrooms with natural light may benefit from the addition of a grow light. Most herbs and flower bulbs perform best with moderate levels of light, which can easily be achieved with the addition of a small grow light. The 18 W grow light with support stand described in the Windowsill Garden design is a great grow light option for this garden.

MATERIALS

Please read through the entire build guide before purchasing the materials.

PREPARATION

1 Install the bidet according to the manufacturer's instructions. It is much easier to install and test the bidet for leaks without a garden and support shelf in the way.

2 Build and install the above-toilet shelf according to the manufacturer's instructions. Measure the width and height of your toilet before purchasing an above-toilet support shelf to ensure it will fit. Select a shelf with a high weight capacity and firmly attach the shelf to the wall for stability. The weight capacity of the shelf used in this design is 75 pounds.

3 Secure the support shelf to a stud in the wall behind the toilet. The weight of the finished garden can reach 50 pounds or more, so it is important to secure the shelf to the wall to avoid it potentially tipping over. This support shelf comes with a heavy-duty zip tie to connect the shelf to a mount screwed into a wall stud.

ITEM	QUANTITY	DIMENSIONS
SUPPORT SHELF		
Above-toilet storage shelf	1	26¾ in L x 8 ⅜ in W x 37 in H
IRRIGATION		
Handheld bidet kit with T-valve, stainless steel holster, and 5-foot stainless steel hose	1	
½-inch stainless steel ball valve weldless bulkhead	1	½-inch bulkhead fitting, ⅞-inch hole
½-inch black vinyl tubing	1	30 in L
GROWING CONTAINER		
Brushed stainless steel planter	1	16 in L x 8 in W x 6 in H
SUBSTRATE		
Marble chips, ½ cubic feet, average rock size 2 to 4 inches	½ cubic feet	
Marble nuggets	5 lb	
OPTIONAL ADDITIONS		
Water-level indicator buoy	1	3¾ inches deep 6½ inches total height
Stainless steel support stakes for flowers	5	16 in H

TOOLS

Drill	⅞-inch bimetal hole saw drill bit	Marker	Measuring Cup (500 mL)	Safety Goggles
Work gloves				

4 The bidet holster can be mounted to the wall, toilet, or shelf depending on your preference.

5 Position the stainless steel planter on the support shelf to identify the desired location of the drain spout. Test to see if the drain spout will block the toilet bowl lid from fully opening. Test to see if the drain spout will be in the way of anyone using the toilet. Test to see if the drain spout is positioned high enough in the planter that the fittings on the bulkhead can properly tighten without contacting the bottom of the planter. Mark the location of the center of the drain spout on the planter with a marker.

SETTING UP THE GROWING CONTAINER

1 If the growing container includes rubber feet, attach them according to the manufacturer's instructions.

2 Drill a ⅞-inch hole in the stainless steel planter at the marked drain spout location from the preparation phase. Drilling through stainless steel is not easy; don't be surprised to see sparks flying from the drill site. Wear gloves and eye protection. Carefully remove any metal fragments after drilling.

3 Install the ½-inch stainless steel ball valve bulkhead in the ⅞-inch hole. Tighten the bulkhead to ensure there is a watertight seal on the planter.

4 Test fill the planter with water to see if there are any leaks at the bulkhead. If there are any leaks, remove the bulkhead and clean the surface around the ⅞-inch hole. Reinstall the bulkhead and test again for leaks. If there are still leaks it may be necessary to use a silicone sealant suitable for metal surfaces.

5 Fill the growing container with large marble chips up to 4 inches from the top of the container. Using large marble chips to fill the bottom portion of the planter helps minimize the risk of small rocks clogging the drain spout. Be sure to be mindful to place only large chips directly around the drain spout.

6 Rinse the marble chips until the water draining from the growing container is clear of sand or dirt. This garden can be filled with marble chips, river rock, expanded clay pellets, or lava rock but no matter what your substrate selection is, it is a good idea to rinse the substrate before adding plants.

7 In a separate container rinse the small marble nuggets. These will be used for the top layer in the garden.

8 Move the growing container onto the support shelf above the toilet. Fill the growing container with water until the water is just slightly above the large marble chips. Use a measuring cup when filling to determine the total water volume required to fill the growing container to the desired fill height. Knowing the volume of water required makes it easier to measure the correct amount of fertilizer required for the garden.

IMPORTANT DETAILS

→ Over the first couple weeks it is important to add water to maintain a full water level that brings the nutrient solution just above the large marble chips but below the surface of the small marble nuggets. After a couple weeks, most plants can tolerate or will benefit from lower water levels.

→ Drain and refill the bathroom garden with a fresh hydroponic nutrient solution every month to maintain adequate nutrients for plant growth and prevent nutrient deficiencies or toxicities.

→ Flower bulbs can be started directly in the garden or in smaller cups until they show visible root growth.

→ Tall flowers can be supported with stainless steel flower stakes to keep them upright.

→ It is unlikely flower bulbs with have multiple blooms when grown in low light conditions. Remove flower bulbs after they bloom and discard or transplant bulbs to an outdoor garden to allow them to replenish their reserves stored in the bulb.

→ If light levels in the bathroom are not sufficient for plant growth (less than 50 umol/m2/s PPFD) it will be necessary to add a grow light. A grow light with a support structure similar to the one shown in the Windowsill Garden described earlier in section 3 is a great option.

9 The optional water-level gauge is easiest to install at this point, but it can also be installed later. The water level indicator should be positioned to display "Full" when the water level is just above the large marble chips but below the small marble nuggets.

10 Transplant flower bulbs, cuttings, or seedlings using the small marble nuggets to secure them in position. It is easier to position flower bulbs, cuttings, and seedlings in the garden before adding the top layer of small marble nuggets. The bottoms of the bulbs or seedlings should make contact with the water just above the large marble chips (which should correspond with the water-level indicator displaying Full). Cuttings should be transplanted deeper in the garden. For delicate cuttings it may be necessary to remove some of the large marble chips when transplanting to avoid damaging their stems. The top layer of small marble nuggets should be ½ to 1 inch deep to secure transplants firmly in position and to block any light from reaching the nutrient solution below. If the top layer is too shallow there will likely be algae development on the surface of the garden.

CROP SELECTION

This garden has limited crop options if it's positioned in a location with low light levels. In locations with high light levels or if you're using a grow light there are many more options. Following are just some of the crops that work well in this garden.

LOW LIGHT (50–150 UMOL/M²/S PPFD) OPTIONS
Flower Bulbs: Paperwhites ('Ziva', 'Nir'), Amaryllis, Tulips, Crocus, Hyacinths, Muscari, Daffodils, Oxalis

Houseplants: Pothos, Goldfish Plants, Spider Plants (*Chlorophytum comosum*), English Ivy, Philodendrons

MODERATE/HIGH LIGHT (150+ UMOL/M2/S PPFD) OPTIONS
Houseplants: Coleus, Papyrus (*Cyperus papyrus*), Lucky Bamboo, Venus Flytrap

Herbs: Mint, Lemon Balm

Paperwhites are one of the easiest flower bulbs to grow indoors and they are very fragrant!

Venus flytraps have low fertilizer requirements and grow well in a consistently wet root zone.

THE NUTS AND BOLTS OF MAINTENANCE

IRRIGATION: Follow the Reservoir Management irrigation strategy detailed in section 4 on page 164.

CROPS: See the Crop Selection section on page 177 earlier in this build guide.

SOIL-BASED OPTION: Use traditional soil-filled garden pots and place them inside the stainless steel planter on a shallow layer of marble chips just high enough to cover the drain spout. Completely drain the planter after watering soil-filled garden pots.

11 Attach the ½-inch black vinyl tubing to the drain spout and completely drain the growing container into the toilet.

12 Fill the garden with a low strength hydroponic nutrient solution (EC 1.0–1.4 mS/cm) to a height just above the large marble chips. Use the water volume measurement from step 8 to determine the amount of fertilizer required to create a low-strength nutrient solution. Use the water level indicator to gauge water height or to remove some of the top layer of small marble nuggets to visually check water level.

POSSIBLE DRAWBACKS

Although this system rarely needs to be cleaned out, when it does need to be cleaned it is messy and time intensive. There are limited crop options that work in this garden without supplemental light.

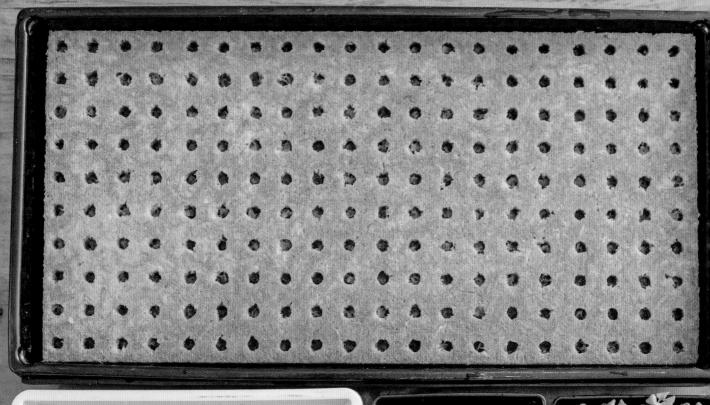

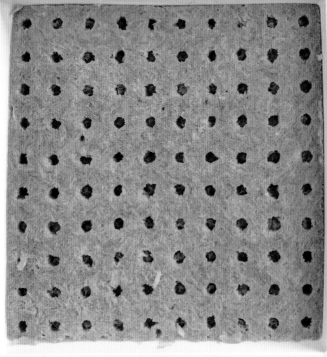

SYSTEM OPERATION

PROPAGATION

PROPAGATION IS A BROAD TERM that includes many methods for starting plants including seeds, cuttings, tissue culture, and root divisions. The exact moment at which propagation ends is clear in some systems but in others there is no clear transition between propagation and grow out.

BASIC STEPS

1. Prepare the substrate.
2. Add seeds or cuttings.
3. Mist seeds or cuttings.
4. Add a humidity dome.
5. Place in a location with adequate light and appropriate temperatures.
6. Irrigate as necessary.

Most of the common propagation problems occur in step 5 (selecting an appropriate location) and step 6 (proper irrigation). When selecting a location, it is important there is sufficient light and appropriate temperatures for the selected crops. Determining when to irrigate will depend on the substrate selection. See the specific irrigation recommendations by method and substrate in the more detailed guides throughout this section.

Three popular tray dimensions used for propagation are 10 in W x 20 in L (also called a 1020), 10 in W x 10 in L and 5 in W x 5 in L. The smaller trays are great for small home hydroponic gardens but the majority of hydroponic propagation equipment including lighting, heat pads and humidity domes are designed for a standard 1020 tray.

STARTING SEEDLINGS

Seedling quality can make or break a hydroponic system. A healthy seedling transplanted into a less-than-ideal hydroponics system can likely survive long enough to reach a harvestable size while a weak seedling transplanted into an amazing hydroponic system may still fail to grow to a harvestable size.

Some systems don't require seedlings (see the Lift Top Coffee Table in section 3 on page 108), and some systems are capable of growing a plant all the way from seed to harvest (see the Stream of Greens in section 3 on page 54), but other systems are very dependent on healthy seedling transplants to perform as expected (see the Lettuce Locker in section 3 on page 140). Growing healthy seedlings is, unfortunately, one of the most challenging parts of hydroponics and gardening in general. Of the many options for starting seedlings, I believe the easiest, most beginner-friendly option is starting seedlings in a floating raft tray with a polymer-based plug. Another popular method is to start seedlings in stone wool. Let's discuss both of these options.

FLOATING RAFT TRAY WITH POLYMER-BASED PLUG (GLUE PLUG)

A floating raft tray with polymer-based plugs can not only grow seedlings, it can grow leafy greens and herbs to a mature harvestable size! This method of growing plants is low maintenance and reliable; it's by far one of my favorite ways to grow plants hydroponically.

Substrate: A polymer-based plug is typically made from peat and/or coco coir bound together with a polymer glue. These products are sometimes referred to as "glue plugs." Polymer-based plugs are typically sold prewetted since they are difficult to rewet if they dry out. Polymer-based plugs are very beginner friendly as they are difficult to overwater; in fact, in a floating raft seedling tray, the polymer-based plugs make constant contact with water. The raft shown in these images fits a 1¼ in. W x 1¼ in. H plug but different sized plug holes are available.

Irrigation Strategy: Fill the tray with a nutrient solution made from standard hydroponic fertilizer. Target an EC of 1.2–1.6 mS/cm or follow the mixing rate recommended by the fertilizer manufacturer for seedlings or young plants. Maintain enough nutrient solution in the tray to keep the raft afloat. I recommended dumping, rinsing, and refilling the nutrient solution in the base tray once per month if you're growing seedlings more than one month.

STONE WOOL SHEET IN NESTED 1020 TRAYS

A stone wool seedling sheet in nested 1020 trays is likely the most common method used to start hydroponic seedlings by both home and commercial growers. Stone wool is very clean and, unlike polymer-based plugs, it can be stored in open air for long periods without worry of the plugs drying

STARTING SEEDLINGS DIRECTLY IN THE GARDEN

Depending on the system design, it may be possible to start seedlings directly in a garden without a specialized propagation system. Starting seedlings in the Stream of Greens and several other gardens described in section 5 on page 54 follow a process very similar to the process of starting seedlings in the floating raft tray with polymer-based plug. Ensure the unseeded plug makes contact with the nutrient solution and then add seeds to the surface of the plug. Lightly mist the seeds and place a clear cup over the plug to create a high humidity environment. For the first few weeks maintain a water level in the garden high enough to make contact with bottoms of the recently seeded plugs. Most crops grow quickly enough to extend their root system into the nutrient solution within three weeks to continue to pull up water even if the water level drops to a level below the plug itself but slow-growing varieties may require a higher water level for longer periods.

Don't underestimate the impact of seeds per plug. For crops such as butterhead lettuce, a single pellet seed is ideal to yield a large, well-formed lettuce head. For crops such as upland cress, a high number of seeds per plug can significantly reduce the amount of time required to grow a large harvestable crop. With fruiting crops such as tomatoes, too many seeds per plug can create a lot of competition between plants, resulting in stretchy, weak growth. With microgreens, a seeding density that's too high often results in mold development in the undercanopy and/or rotting seedlings.

IRRIGATION STRATEGY

How: Remove the top 1020 tray with drainage and partially fill the lower, nondraining 1020 tray with a hydroponic nutrient solution. Slowly dip the top 1020 tray holding the stone wool sheet into the nutrient solution and let it rest for 5 minutes. If the sheet absorbs all of the nutrient solution, add some more and repeat. Remove the top tray and let it drip drain for a few minutes. Dump any remaining nutrient solution from the bottom tray. Nest the top tray back into the bottom tray until the next irrigation event.

When: There are several ways to determine when to irrigate stone wool including touching the surface or digital meters, but the most reliable and my preferred method for new growers is manually checking the weight of the stone wool sheet to target a drop to 33–40 percent water content between irrigations. Use the following steps to measure water content:

out or diminishing in quality. The quality of a seedling started in stone wool is tied closely to the timing of irrigations; allow enough time for the substrate to dry between irrigations while not waiting too long to the point of damaging the plants.

Substrate: Stone wool is a popular insulation material in construction. Internationally this substrate is typically called stone wool while in the United States it is commonly called rockwool. Put simply, stone wool is made from molten rocks (think lava) spun into strands like cotton candy. Wearing gloves is recommended when handling stone wool. Before seeding in stone wool, place it in a tray with drainage, rinse the substrate with water, and then drench it with a hydroponic nutrient solution mixed at a strength appropriate for seedlings (see Fertilizer Management on page 164). The two most common stone wool sizes are 25/40 and 36/40. These size descriptions reference its width (25 mm or 36 mm) and height (40 mm). All of the stone wool plugs shown in this section are 25/40s (1 in W x 1.57 in H).

Some seeds perform best with a topcoat of vermiculite, coco coir, or other fine substrate to hold moisture around the seeds and provide some weight on top of the seeds to help push the young roots into the stone wool. After applying a topcoat, it is important to mist or irrigate from above to fully saturate the topcoat.

This tray with a stone wool sheet weighs 462 grams when dry and 3,734 grams when it's fully saturated. The total water weight when saturated is 3,272 grams, which is 3,734 grams (wet) minus 462 grams (dry). Seedlings started in this tray should be irrigated only when the weight drops down below 1,771 grams, which is 3,272 grams (water weight) multiplied by 40 percent (target water content) plus 462 grams (dry tray weight). For this tray I would try not to let the dry down weight drop below 1,542 grams or a target water content of 33 percent.

Seedlings started in stone wool can be transplanted as soon as their roots emerge from the bottom of the plug. Try to transplant stone wool seedlings before the roots from seedlings in one plug grow into neighboring plugs.

Don't be afraid to thin out seedlings before transplanting! Overcrowded plants may not develop properly. See the Crop Selection Charts in the appendix on page 177 for the recommended number of seedlings per plug.

1. Weigh the tray with a dry stone wool sheet.

2. Weigh the tray with the fully saturated stone wool sheet minutes after the tray stops dripping from its initial soak.

3. Subtract the weight obtained in step 1 from the weight measured in step 2 to determine the weight just of the water in the stone wool sheet.

4. Multiply the number from step 3 by 40 percent to determine the target dry down water weight

Waiting to irrigate until reaching this dry down target helps minimize algae development on the surface of stone wool and improves root development. The weight of the seedlings themselves is minimal compared to the weight of water in the stone wool sheet so don't worry about calculating a new target dry down weight as crops mature and increase in weight themselves. The initial calculated dry down target can be used for many weeks. Experienced growers will become familiar with the weight of the tray simply by lifting it and can determine when to irrigate without weighing the tray on a scale but for new growers, it is a good idea to manually weigh the tray for the first few irrigations. Don't be alarmed if it takes six or more days for a stone wool sheet to dry down to the target weight between irrigations. The specific dry down time will depend on local conditions and crop maturity.

If you're interested in learning how to start microgreen seeds in your growing system, please visit my website for specific growing instructions for these plants: www.FarmerTyler.com/blog/microgreens.

HEAT PADS

If you're growing in a cold environment, a heat pad can significantly reduce the time required to germinate seeds or develop roots on a cutting. Heat pads are available in many sizes including skinny pads sized for windowsills. Many seed packets include a recommended temperature range for germination. For the temperature range recommendations to germinate popular hydroponic crops see the Crop Selection Charts in the appendix on page 177.

STARTING CUTTINGS

Some crops are much easier to propagate from a cutting instead of a seed. Plants such as mint can be grown from seed, but the development process is slow and it can be very difficult to find seeds for a specific desired variety (e.g., chocolate mint). See the Crop Selection Charts in the appendix on page 177 for the preferred propagation method (seeds or cuttings) for popular hydroponic crops.

There are several popular methods for rooting cuttings and each has its pros and cons. For beginners I recommend starting cuttings in a deep-water culture or aeroponic system. These methods have a much higher success rate, and the process is more straightforward. The drawback of these methods is that the cuttings are bare root, meaning they have no substrate such as stone wool surrounding the roots. Handling and transplanting bare-root seedlings can be challenging depending on the garden design but in my opinion, this challenge is a smaller hurdle toward success than starting a healthy cutting in a stone wool plug. Whether one is rooting a cutting in stone wool, deep water culture, or an aeroponic garden, the process of taking and preparing the cutting is the same.

TAKING AND PREPARING CUTTINGS

1 Take a cutting from the mother plant. When possible, select cuttings with thicker stems branching off from the base of the plant. Make the cut just above the internodes on the mother plant to limit the amount of excess stem remaining on the mother plant, which will likely die and rot.

2 Clean the cutting. A fresh cutting with no root system will struggle to supply the moisture required to maintain a large canopy. Remove all but a few leaves on the cutting.

3 Make an angled cut at the base of the cutting to maximize the area for new root development.

STARTING CUTTINGS IN DEEP WATER CULTURE OR AN AEROPONIC GARDEN

1 Use a foam plug or collar to secure the cuttings in place.

2 For deep water culture, ensure the water level is high enough to make contact with at least 1 inch of the stem.

3 Check for root development after one week.

4 Determining when a cutting is ready for transplant can be difficult. The safest option is to wait until the cutting develops new leaves, but this can take three or more weeks. Most cuttings are safe to transplant before they develop new leaves but the success of newly rooted cuttings after transplant depends on the hydroponic garden design.

STARTING CUTTINGS IN STONE WOOL

1 Prepare the substrate. Soak the stone wool plugs in a hydroponic nutrient solution.

2 Dibble the substrate to minimize the resistance on the stems when inserting the cuttings into the substrate. A chopstick, pencil, and pen are all good options for creating a dibble hole.

3 Add the cuttings to the substrate.

4 Mist the cuttings and add a humidity dome.

5 Irrigate with a low-strength hydroponic nutrient solution when the substrate feels lightweight (see Stone Wool Sheet in Nested 1020 Trays in this section on page 160 for an example).

6 Check for root development. Most popular crops for hydroponics propagated from cuttings develop roots within two to three weeks.

7 Once roots are visible, gradually start acclimatizing the freshly rooted cuttings to a lower humidity by opening vents on the humidity dome for a couple days.

8 Transplant the cuttings into the hydroponic garden.

These mint cuttings were rooted in the Lift Top Coffee Table deep water culture garden from section 3 on page 108.

FERTILIZER MAINTENANCE

This section covers the nuts and bolts of fertilizer maintenance for specific applications; for a general review of hydroponic fertilizer fundamentals, key terms, and recommended equipment please see Nutrients in section 2 on page 23.

Modern retail hydroponic fertilizers are very user friendly and are designed to support healthy plant growth even in extreme conditions. With commercial hydroponic fertilizers, I closely monitor pH and the nutrient analysis. But with my home hydroponic gardens operating on retail fertilizers designed for new growers, I am nowhere near as vigilant, sometimes never even measuring EC or pH once throughout the grow cycle. For new growers, a somewhat lazy approach to fertilizer management might actually be beneficial as I usually see more issues from overmanaging the nutrient solution. It is easy to get excited by all of the potential fertilizer amendments available for hydroponics—I have a pantry full of hydroponic fertilizer products—but more is rarely better. When it comes to hydroponic fertilizers, I've killed far more plants with too much love than I've killed with a little bit of neglect.

FERTILIZER MAINTENANCE BY SYSTEM TYPE

Refer to the following table for irrigation strategy recommended by system type.

DIY SYSTEM	IRRIGATION STRATEGY
Suction Cup Planters	C
Windowsill Garden	C *See Note
Salad Bowl	A
Stream of Greens	A
Bar Cart	C
Bar Tower	A
Dinner Table	C
Picture Frame	A
Corner Shelf	A
Lift Top Coffee Table	A
End Table	B
Cabinet Farm	C
Lettuce Locker	A
Bathroom Flower Garden	A
1020 Tray with Floating Raft	A

*The Windowsill Garden has a very small reservoir below the stone wool blocks enabling it to use irrigation strategy A, but due to the increased risk of nutrient accumulation in a small reservoir over time, I recommend operating this garden using irrigation strategy C.

TYPE A—RESERVOIR MANAGEMENT

Irrigation strategy A, which I describe as reservoir management, is designed for systems that are filled with a standard hydroponic nutrient solution at startup and then topped-off with a low-strength nutrient solution between system flushes/cleanings.

Startup: Mix fertilizer into potable water at either the strength recommended on the fertilizer packaging or a target EC listed in the table at the end of this chapter on page 166.

Top-Off Nutrient Solution: As plants uptake water from the reservoir it will be necessary to add water to maintain a target water level, typically high enough to maintain contact with seedlings or in systems with pumps at least 75 percent full. To avoid nutrient accumulation and an excessive EC rise over time, use a lower-strength nutrient solution when making additions to reservoir. I typically use a nutrient solution at about 75 percent the strength of the nutrient solution used at system startup. For example, if I'm using an EC meter, I might use a nutrient solution with an

Never add a dry powder fertilizer directly into a reservoir. It is important to fully dissolve dry powder fertilizer in a separate container before pouring the mix into a hydroponic garden.

EC of 1.6 mS/cm at startup and 1.2 mS/cm for top-offs. If I'm not using an EC meter and mixing by weight, I might use 1 tsp. per gallon at startup and ¾ tsp. per gallon for top-offs.

Flushing: Depending on the garden design, it may be possible to go many months without fully flushing (or removing) and refilling with a new nutrient solution. The best method for determining when to flush a hydroponic system involves lab analysis of the nutrient solution and some stoichiometry calculations that are beyond the scope of this home hydroponics book. For new growers I recommend using the following rule of thumb to calculate a conservative approximation for when to flush a hydroponic reservoir: Flush the reservoir and refill with a new nutrient solution when the total volume of top-offs equals the initial volume of nutrient solution used at startup. For example, a hydroponic garden with a 100 gallon reservoir that requires a top-off addition of 10 gallons per week would require a full system flush after 10 weeks (10 gallons x 10 weeks = 100 gallons).

TYPE B—DRAIN-TO-WASTE

A drain-to-waste garden receives fresh nutrient solution at each irrigation with a portion of that nutrient solution draining away (or leaching) from the soilless substrate. This irrigation method avoids nutrient accumulations and deficiencies by providing a fresh well-balanced nutrient solution at every irrigation. Typically, the target EC for nutrient solutions used in a

drain-to-waste garden is lower than the target EC for the same crop grown in a typical reservoir styled hydroponic garden. When irrigating a drain-to-waste garden aim for a leachate volume that is approximately 10–25 percent of the delivered nutrient solution volume.

TYPE C—NO RESERVOIR AND NO LEACHATE

Hydroponic gardens using this irrigation strategy can be challenging as there is nowhere for excess nutrient solution to drain and all nutrients added are either taken up by the plants or accumulate in the substrate. The nutrient accumulation with this technique can be mitigated with a few techniques.

REMOVE, DIP, AND DRIP

This method is best for gardens with small and easy-to-move crops such as the Dinner Table or Bar Cart garden projects. When the substrate feels lightweight or is dry to the touch, remove the crop from the garden and dip the substrate into a nutrient solution. After soaking in the nutrient solution for 30 seconds, remove the crop and let the nutrient solution drip away from the substrate for a few minutes before returning the crop to the garden.

SOAK, RISE, AND RINSE

This method is best for gardens with crops that are moderately difficult to remove, such as the Suction Cup Planters design. When starting the garden soak the substrate in a nutrient solution mixed to a standard drain-to-waste strength. For subsequent irrigations use a small volume of one-quarter strength nutrient solution (relative to initial soak) when the surface of the substrate feels dry to the touch or, if you're using a sensor,

when the moisture content drops below 50 percent. Add nutrient solution slowly when irrigating to minimize the amount of excess nutrient solution pooling under the substrate. Over time some nutrients will accumulate or rise to levels harmful to the crop, necessitating a rinse. The exact frequency of rinses will depend on local conditions, crop maturity, and many other factors, but generally a rinse once per month is sufficient to remove any excessive nutrient accumulation. For rinsing I bring crops from the garden to a sink and run water over the substrate for 30 seconds, which is about enough water to fully saturate the substrate several times. After the rinse, repeat the process used to start the garden beginning with soaking the substrate in a nutrient solution mixed to a standard drain-to-waste strength.

SLOW MARCH

This method is not ideal but it's sometimes necessary when gardens have crops that are very difficult or impossible to remove for irrigation. The process is the same as the previous Soak, Rise, and Rinse method, but instead of rinsing the substrate the nutrients are simply allowed to accumulate over time in a slow march toward dangerously high levels that will negatively impact growth. To make the slow march even slower, it is possible to replace the one-quarter strength nutrient solution with plain water for some irrigations, but this may slow down crop growth as well.

An EC meter enables a gardener to monitor the fertilizer concentration in the hydroponic nutrient solution. While it is possible to operate a hydroponic garden without an EC meter, the information that a gardener can gather from the use of an EC meter may enable alternative fertilizer management techniques beyond periodic flushes and refills of the garden's reservoir.

FERTILIZER RATE RECOMMENDATIONS

It is possible to achieve healthy crop growth using nutrient solutions with EC measurements outside of the target ranges listed below. The following EC targets are general recommendations that do not consider all of the factors present in the specific garden that affect the fertilizer requirements including specific crop variety, crop maturity, light levels and climate.

| CROP | TARGET EC RANGE (MS/CM) | |
	A—RESERVOIR MANAGEMENT	B—DRAIN-TO-WASTE
Seedlings and Microgreens	1.0–1.8	0.7–1.5
Leafy Greens and Herbs	1.4–2.0	1.0–1.6
Tomatoes and Flowering Crops	1.6–2.4	1.4–2.0
Mixed Crops	1.6–2.0	1.4–1.6

*The following EC targets are based on a typical municipal water source with an incoming EC of 0.3 mS/cm. If the source water has an EC above 0.5 mS/cm, it may be difficult to manage the nutrients without frequent flushes. If the source water has an EC above 1 mS/cm, it may be necessary to use a reverse-osmosis filter or other filtration equipment to lower incoming EC.

The following table can be used to approximate the expected EC with a standard one-part dry hydroponic fertilizer mixed into distilled water, deionized water, or water treated with a reverse osmosis filter. Most municipal water sources in the United States will increase the expected EC by 0.2–0.4 mS/cm.

| DRY 10-5-14 OR 5-15-14 HYDROPONIC FERTILIZER | |
RATE PER GALLON	EXPECTED EC (MS/CM)
¼ tsp.	0.3–0.5
½ tsp.	0.7–1.0
1 tsp.	1.4–1.9
1¼ tsp.	1.8–2.3
1½ tsp.	2.2–2.8
2 tsp.	2.7–3.2

SYSTEM CLEANING

WHEN TO CLEAN

Many factors affect the required cleaning frequency of the growing containers including plant maturity, water temperature, water quality, and container size. While there is a simple rule-of-thumb method for determining when to flush a hydroponic reservoir, it is less easy to define the frequency at which a hydroponic garden requires a deep cleaning. In almost all cases (besides some organic hydroponic gardens) frequent cleanings are best to minimize the risk of plant pathogens harming the crop. But to clean a system properly with cleaning chemicals it is usually necessary to remove all plants from the garden. Cleaning a hydroponic garden once per month is great when it's feasible, but I typically try to clean my gardens as little as possible to minimize the risk of damaging plants in the process and, more importantly, I'm lazy. To determine when a deep cleaning is absolutely necessary, check for the following signs:

Smell

Smells that indicate a hydroponic garden should be cleaned could be described as either fishy or vegetable soup. The ocean-seaweed-fishy smell is usually a sign of algae growth in a standard hydroponic garden or it may be the smell of the fertilizer inputs in an organic hydroponic garden. A vegetable soup smell generally indicates plant material and other organic matter are decomposing in the garden.

Slime

Biofilms, the dark slime on reservoir surfaces, are common in hydroponic gardens and usually do not necessitate a deep cleaning. Biofilms are most problematic in aeroponic and hydroponic gardens with small irrigation lines and emitters that can be easily clogged from the biofilms. Biofilms can develop quickly in warm environments. Some microbial inoculants designed for hydroponics can help break down biofilms, but the best way to remove them is a deep clean. My preferred cleaning chemical for removing biofilms from irrigation lines is outdoor bleach. Standard household bleach can work as well but outdoor bleach includes a surfactant that, in my experience, greatly helps remove stubborn biofilms from difficult-to-access surfaces.

Systems with heavy, difficult-to-remove reservoirs may be easier to drain and clean with a wet/dry shop vacuum.

HOW TO CLEAN

1 Remove the plants.

2 Save any expanded clay pellets; these can be cleaned and reused.

3 Drain the system reservoir.

4 Scrub off any debris from surfaces. If you're unable to scrub away debris, it may be necessary to proceed to the next step and scrub again after using a cleaning chemical to loosen debris from the surfaces.

5 Sanitize the surfaces with a cleaning chemical. To sanitize irrigation lines, it is necessary to fill the reservoir with a diluted cleaning chemical and pump it through the system. Scrub surfaces again after applying cleaning chemical. See table below for cleaning chemical options.

6 Check system surfaces for any signs of remaining debris or biofilms; if any are present, repeat steps 4 and 5.

7 Rinse any cleaning chemicals from surface of growing system. For systems with irrigation lines, fill the reservoir with clean water and run the pump to rinse out the irrigation lines. It may be necessary to dump out the water, refill with fresh water, and rinse the system multiple times to ensure there are no cleaning chemicals remaining in system; two or three rinses is typically sufficient to remove most cleaning chemicals. The most common visual sign of remaining cleaning chemical residues in the system are bubbles.

8 Your hydroponic garden is clean!

Besides the growing container, it is important to regularly clean the fans and grow light surfaces.

CHEMICAL	RATE	NOTES
Dish soap		Great for most systems with easily accessible surfaces. Dish soap is not ideal for use in systems with irrigation lines or difficult-to-access parts as it is unlikely to remove biofilms if it's not paired with physical scrubbing.
Isopropyl alcohol	70% or stronger	Good for sanitizing surfaces.
Hydrogen peroxide	3%	A popular commercial option for commercial hydroponic growers. There are many horticultural hydrogen peroxide products available to gardeners. Hydrogen peroxide can sanitize surfaces and has some ability to loosen organic matter from surfaces, enabling it to clean difficult-to-access irrigation line.
Quaternary ammonium chloride salts	*1 tbs/gallon	*Rates vary based on specific product used.
Bleach	½–1 ounce per gallon, or 1:10 dilution with 5¼% household bleach	A great option but bleach should be handled with care to avoid fumes or excessively high rates that can damage surfaces. Bleach can both sanitize surfaces and loosen organic matter from surfaces. Bleach is a very popular cleaning chemical used by commercial hydroponic growers.
Outdoor Bleach	1/2–1 ounce per gallon	One of the strongest options. Great for removing stubborn debris and stains. Capable of removing biofilms in irrigation lines. Generates a lot of foam, which may overflow from the reservoir; use with caution. Wear gloves and eye protection and use in well ventilated areas. Requires multiple rinses to fully remove from system.

PLANT HEALTH

The root causes of plant health issues can be very difficult to identify. In many cases a combination of factors leads to a problem. For example, tip burn on lettuce can be linked to low calcium in the nutrient solution, high humidity, or high light levels, and in some cases each of these factors viewed individually may fall within an acceptable range but when pulled together, they create a situation ideal for tip burn. For this reason it can be very difficult to correctly identify the root causes of plant health issues. With experience it is possible to see how the many factors in a growing environment may interact to create a problem, but for new growers feeling lost in the diagnoses, following are some of the most common problems and their solutions.

BROWN MUSHY ROOTS

Brown mushy roots typically indicate the presence of a root rot pathogen in a hydroponic garden. Surprisingly most hydroponic gardens have some root rot pathogen spores present at all times but if plants are healthy, they may not be very susceptible to infection. Root rot outbreaks require not only the presence of root rot pathogens, they require favorable environmental conditions (e.g., warm water temperature, low dissolved oxygen) and a susceptible crop (e.g., stressed, damaged).

Limit Sources of Root Rot Pathogens Risk Factors

→ Dirty water source. Great sources included reverse-osmosis filtered and rainwater. Most municipal water sources are also well suited for hydroponics. Well water, pond water, and water from streams are higher risk.

→ Dirty substrate. Organic substrates such as coco coir, peat, and potting mixes are the highest risks. Engineered substrates such as stone wool and foam sponges are the cleanest substrate options.

→ Dirty fertilizer. Organic fertilizers are typically low risk for introducing root rot pathogens, but they do typically introduce organic matter into the system, which can increase the risk of creating anaerobic conditions in the reservoir which creates a more favorable condition for a root rot infection.

Limit Conditions Favorable to Root Rot Pathogens

→ Warm water. This is an especially high risk if the temperature is greater than 80 degrees F.

→ Low dissolved oxygen. This is an especially high risk if the crop has root oxygen requirements and the water is stagnant (no aeration or circulation of nutrient solution).

Limit Crop's Susceptibility

→ Avoid stressful conditions that could damage the roots like low/high pH, low/high EC, warm water or exposure to cleaning chemicals that were not sufficiently rinsed away during system cleaning.

- ➔ Remove crops damaged from drying out events. Roots drying out is frequently observed in aeroponic towers or any system with irrigation lines that might clog.
- ➔ Avoid susceptible crops. Spinach is one of the most susceptible crops to root rot pathogens.

How to Fix Root Rot Infections

There are many ways to slow a root rot infection but it is nearly impossible to completely cure or eradicate the problem without using strong fungicides/bactericides. The best solution for root rots in a home garden is to remove all plants, deep clean the garden, and replant with clean seedlings.

STRETCHY CROP GROWTH

Stretchy, spindly growth is most often due to inadequate light levels. A crop that is not receiving enough light elongates its stems and leaves to get closer to the light to access as much as it can. The leaves in a crop not receiving sufficient light are typically very delicate. Other potential causes of stretchy crop growth are excessively high planting density leading to competition between plants and very warm air temperatures.

Risk Factors

- ➔ Low light. See the Crop Selection Charts in the appendix on page 177 for recommended light levels for popular hydroponic crops.
- ➔ Excessively high planting density creates a scenario similar to low light levels, which causes the crop to stretch toward the light to outcompete neighboring plants as there is insufficient light to meet all of their needs.
- ➔ High air temperature.

How to Fix Stretchy Crop Growth

While a plant can switch from stretchy growth to compact growth, there is no way to revert the growth that has already occurred. For some crops it may be possible to harvest the stretchy parts of the crop and then remedy the risk factors leading to the stretchy growth by reducing planting density or adding more light to ensure future growth develops normally. Typically the best course of action is to restart the garden with new plants and provide adequate light for the crops during their entire lives to get nice, compact, healthy growth from the start.

Stretchy top growth and elongated stems can occur when light levels are too low.

Tip burn often occurs on new growth.

TIP BURN

Tip burn is most frequently seen on mature lettuce crops but almost all crops are susceptible. There are many types of tip burn but the specific one described here occurs on new growth such as the developing leaves emerging from the center of a lettuce head. These leaves are growing fast and require calcium to build cell walls. Unfortunately calcium transport through a plant is a relatively slow process that struggles to keep up with the demand, especially when faced with the following risk factors.

Risk Factors

- → Low calcium in the nutrient solution.
- → Low humidity.
- → High humidity.
- → Poor airflow through crop canopy. This can be the result of the crop canopy being too dense or simply the lack of any equipment to encourage airflow.
- → Very high light levels.
- → Very susceptible crops. Some varieties, such as 'Flashy Trout Back' lettuce (shown above), are very susceptible to tip burn and typically show symptoms far earlier than other lettuce varieties.

Interveinal chlorosis on new growth is typically a sign of an iron deficiency.

How to Fix Tip Burn

There is no cure for leaves that already have tip burn but it is possible to limit future tip burn by minimizing its risk factors.

LEAF YELLOWING (CHLOROSIS)

Leaf yellowing, or chlorosis, is the loss of chlorophyll in leaves. There are many reasons why a plant might display chlorosis including senescence, or the natural leaf death observed as a crop grows old. The location (young or old leaves) and pattern (e.g., spotting along veins and along leaf edges) of the chlorosis provide a lot of information on the cause of the chlorosis.

New Growth Leaf Yellowing Risk Factors

- → An old nutrient solution that has insufficient iron for the crop.
- → A crop, such as basil, that has high iron demand or is classified as 'iron inefficient.'
- → The nutrient solution pH is outside of the target range.
- → General imbalance of nutrients in nutrient solution, typically as a result of excessive phosphorus.

Mature/Lower Leaf Yellowing Risk Factors

➜ Low nitrogen levels.

➜ Root damage.

➜ An old crop displaying natural senescence with yellowing and eventual death of its lower leaves.

How to Fix Chlorosis

The preceding two examples of chlorosis are the most common seen by hydroponic growers but there are other ways chlorosis might present in a crop. My first step after observing chlorosis is to check the roots for damage and scout through the canopy for pests. If I can rule out root damage and pests, then the cause is likely related to the nutrient solution; in that case, it is best to flush the system and refill with a freshly mixed nutrient solution.

WILTING

Wilting is typically associated with a plant not receiving water, but wilting can also occur in hydroponic systems when the plant roots are submerged in water. Wilting is due to a plant's inability to uptake water, which can be due to a lack of water but other factors can inhibit a plant's ability to uptake water including root damage, low dissolved oxygen in the nutrient solution, and high air temperatures with low humidity.

Risk Factors

➜ Lack of water typically due to clogged irrigation lines.

➜ Root damage.

➜ Warm water temperatures.

➜ Inadequate dissolved oxygen in the root zone (often linked to warm water temperatures).

➜ High air temperatures with low humidity. In this case the water is simply moving out of the leaves faster than the roots can bring water in.

How to Fix Wilting

Most plants recover from minor wilting incidences with little immediate visible damage. The repercussions of a wilting incident in a hydroponic garden are typically observed several days later with the development of tip burn and/or patches of chlorosis. Every day for a week after a wilting incident, check the plant roots for signs of root rot and remove any plants showing symptoms. Plants may recover from a wilting incident, but the root damage typically associated with the event increases their risk of being infected with a root rot pathogen that could then quickly spread throughout the garden.

CHLOROSIS AND NECROSIS

Chlorosis is the loss of chlorophyll, the green pigment in leaves; chlorotic leaves appear yellow. Necrosis is the death of plant cells; necrotic leaves appear black or brown. The first sign of most nutrient deficiencies and plant pathogens is chlorosis and over time the chlorotic patches of growth become necrotic.

PEST MANAGEMENT

INTEGRATED PEST MANAGEMENT (IPM)

Pest management is more than just spraying pesticides, it is a holistic approach including prevention, monitoring, and appropriate responses. Prevention involves minimizing entry points for pests, selecting crop varieties less susceptible to pests, and creating an environment that is less attractive to pests. After taking steps to prevent pests from entering a garden, it is important to monitor pest presence using a variety of tools including scouting, sticky traps, and indicator plants. By monitoring pest pressure it is possible to determine if the pest population is growing and if it is necessary to take action to control the pest population. Once a pest is spotted there are many control options. If the pest presence is spotted early it may be possible to control the population using simple mechanical control methods, such as squishing them with your fingers. If a mechanical control is not sufficient, then it may be time to escalate to biological controls. If biological controls are not sufficient, then it may be necessary to escalate to biopesticides. After biopesticides there are chemical pesticide options, but these are not necessary for controlling pest pressure in a typical home hydroponic garden. For more specifics on pest and disease management, please visit my website www.farmertyler.com/homehydroponics/pestmanagement

COMMON PROBLEMS AND TROUBLESHOOTING

My favorite hydroponic systems are simple and difficult to break; unfortunately these systems are usually less popular than the flashier hydroponic systems such as vertical towers, high pressure aeroponics, and systems with moving parts (i.e., Ferris wheels). This book does cover designs for systems with these features because they can indeed be run and are capable of growing plants in visually appealing ways, but they come with an increased risk of system failure. Following are the most common problems seen in hydroponic gardens along with the most susceptible garden designs for each problem.

ALGAE

Algae development occurs on surfaces that are consistently wet and exposed to light. Algae itself is not a major concern as it is unlikely to affect plant health, but algae can be a food source for garden pests such as fungus gnats, which can harm a crop.

Susceptible Systems

All hydroponic gardens.

Remedies

➡ Reduce light exposure to wet surfaces. This could involve using net cup covers as seen in the Picture Frame garden on page 82 or block covers as seen in the Suction Cup Garden design on page 34.

➡ For manually irrigated gardens using large stone wool or coco coir blocks, allow the substrate surface to dry between irrigations. Overwatering is a very common problem that can affect root development and the overall plant growth rate.

BIOFILM

Biofilms are the slime on the insides of reservoirs and irrigation lines. This slime is due to microbes growing in the nutrient solution and clinging to surfaces. Biofilms are generally harmless but in extreme conditions they can clog irrigation lines and/or harbor pathogens.

Susceptible Systems

All hydroponic gardens.

Remedies

→ Add biofilm degrading microbes/enzymes. There are many hydroponic products containing enzymes that help accelerate the breakdown of organic matter such as biofilms.

→ Manually scrub away biofilm from accessible surfaces. If possible, remove the biofilm debris with a sponge or towel.

→ Shut down the garden and perform a deep clean using bleach (especially effective is outdoor bleach) or a strong hydrogen peroxide solution. This method will require a full reset of the hydroponic garden, but it is the most effective method for removing biofilms from difficult-to-access areas such as irrigation lines. See System Cleaning earlier in section 4 on page 167 for more information on cleaning chemical options.

CLOGGED EMITTERS

Hydroponic irrigation tubes and emitters can clog due to excessive biofilms or other particulates in the nutrient solution. A common source of clogs in new hydroponic gardens is plastic shavings from drilling or cutting into pipes. In mature hydroponic gardens the clogs are often due to organic matter.

Susceptible Systems

Bar Tower, Lettuce Locker, and any garden design with irrigation emitters.

Remedies

→ Increase the flow rate if possible. The additional pressure in the irrigation lines can help push through debris and unclog emitters.

→ Turn off the irrigation and push an unfolded paper clip or metal twist tie into the irrigation emitters to loosen debris. Turn on the irrigation to see if clog is fixed. Another, slightly messier option is to push an unfolded paper clip into the emitter while leaving the pump running.

→ Replace the emitter.

→ Deep clean the system. Outdoor bleach products are great for removing organic matter from difficult-to-reach areas that can't easily be scrubbed by hand (such as irrigation lines).

LEAKS

Operating a leaky hydroponic garden can feel like equal parts gardening and plumbing. Quickly fixing, or preferably preventing leaks can help maximize your time gardening and minimize the tome plumbing.

Susceptible Systems

All hydroponic gardens but the most susceptible systems have irrigation designs with pumps and emitters such as the Bar Tower and Lettuce Locker gardens.

Remedies

➡ Tighten fittings if possible.

➡ Plumber's tape has helped me stop many leaks over the years. Wrap the net cup, irrigation barb, gasket fitting, or other leak source with a single layer of plumber's tape to start. If the leak is not fixed try adding a few more layers.

➡ Food contact-approved clear silicone sealant can be used in many of the same applications as plumber's tape, but it is a more permanent solution.

➡ Replace the item that is leaking if it appears the leak is due to a defective item.

➡ If possible, set the irrigation to have a very short on-time that is incapable of releasing enough water during an irrigation event to create a leak. This approach can be seen in the Bar Tower in section 3 on page 66 where a pump timer is set to three seconds on every 30 minutes.

➡ Use a wicking fabric to direct the flow of water. This approach can be seen in the Lettuce Locker in section 3 on page 140 where a fabric lines the back of the tower to encourage water to remain along the back of the tower.

Leaks from the face of the tower coming through plant sites are a common problem in vertical tower gardens.

CONVERSION TABLES

EC TO TDS CONVERSIONS

EC (MS/CM)	CF	PPM 500 (TDS)	PPM 700
0.1	1	50	70
0.2	2	100	140
0.3	3	150	210
0.4	4	200	280
0.5	5	250	350
0.6	6	300	420
0.7	7	350	490
0.8	8	400	560
0.9	9	450	630
1	10	500	700
1.1	11	550	770
1.2	12	600	840
1.3	13	650	910
1.4	14	700	980
1.5	15	750	1050
1.6	16	800	1120
1.7	17	850	1190
1.8	18	900	1260
1.9	19	950	1330
2	20	1000	1400
2.1	21	1050	1470
2.2	22	1100	1540
2.3	23	1150	1610
2.4	24	1200	1680
2.5	25	1250	1750
3	30	1500	2100
3.5	35	1750	2450
4	40	2000	2800
4.5	45	2250	3150
5	50	2500	3500

LUX : PPFD

Multiply lux measurement by the following conversion factors to obtain an **approximate** PPFD (μmol/m2/s). For more accurate PPFD measurements use a PAR meter.

LIGHT SOURCE	CONVERSION FACTOR
Sunlight	0.019
LED, White	0.013–0.019
LED, Red + Blue + White	0.025
LED, Red + Blue	0.089
LED, Blue Only	0.115
LED, Red Only	0.077
Ceramic Metal Halide (3100 K)	0.017
Ceramic Metal Halide (4200 K)	0.015
Fluorescent	0.014
Single-Ended High-Pressure Sodium (SE HPS)	0.012
Double-Ended High-Pressure Sodium (DE HPS)	0.013

Example: A reading of 10,000 lux measured under a fluorescent lamp would be converted to PPFD by multiplying 10,000 lux by the conversion factor 0.014 to get an approximate PPFD of 140 μmol/m2/s.

CROP SELECTION CHARTS

The recommendations in these crop selection charts do not focus on optimal conditions but rather, acceptable conditions. Since it is often difficult to create the optimal conditions for growth in a home hydroponic garden, I believe it is more helpful to know the approximate ranges a crop can tolerate.

LETTUCE AND SALAD GREENS

GERMINATION TEMPERATURE	60–70 degrees F
WATER TEMPERATURE	60–75 degrees F
EC	0.8–2.3 mS/cm
PH	5.5–6.5
AIR TEMPERATURE	60–80 degrees F
HUMIDITY	40–80%
LIGHT INTENSITY	100–650 umol/m2/s
DLI	12–21 mol/m2/d
PHOTOPERIOD	12–20 hours/day
CANOPY HEIGHT	4–8 inches
CANOPY WIDTH	4–8 inches
TYPICAL SPACING	2–9 plants/ft2
ROOT SIZE	Small
ROOT ZONE OXYGEN REQUIREMENTS	Low
GROWING SYSTEMS	Suction Cup Planters, Windowsill Garden, Salad Bowl, Stream of Greens, Bar Cart, Bar Tower, Dinner Table, Picture Frame, Corner Shelf, Coffee Table, End Table, Cabinet Farm, Lettuce Locker, 1020 Tray with Floating Raft

BRASSICACEAE

Brassicaceae includes kale, bok choy, tatsoi, mizuna, mustards, cabbage, radishes, and watercress along with many others! It is amazing how many vegetables are in the *Brassicaceae* family, and traditional breeding efforts have even developed some new variations in the past years including kalettes (a cross of kale and brussel sprouts) and other unique crosses of individuals in the *Brassicaceae* family!

GERMINATION TEMPERATURE	65–75 degrees F
WATER TEMPERATURE	60–75 degrees F
EC	0.8–2.3 mS/cm
PH	5.5–6.5
AIR TEMPERATURE	60–85F
HUMIDITY	40–80%
LIGHT INTENSITY	150 umol/m2/s–650 umol/m2/s
DLI	12–21 mol/m2/d
PHOTOPERIOD	12–18 hours/day
CANOPY HEIGHT	4–10 inches
CANOPY WIDTH	4–8 inches
TYPICAL SPACING	2–9 plants/ft2
ROOT SIZE	Small–Medium
ROOT ZONE OXYGEN REQUIREMENTS	Low–Medium
GROWING SYSTEMS	Suction Cup Planters, Windowsill Garden, Salad Bowl, Stream of Greens, Bar Cart, Bar Tower, Dinner Table, Picture Frame, Corner Shelf, Coffee Table, End Table, Cabinet Farm, Lettuce Locker, 1020 Tray with Floating Raft

BEETS & SWISS CHARD

Red cabbage varieties such as 'Integro' have a nice, thick leaf texture even as a baby green.

AMARANTHACEAE

Amaranthaceae includes vegetable crops such as beets, Swiss chard, and spinach.

BEETS AND SWISS CHARD

GERMINATION TEMPERATURE	70–86 degrees F
WATER TEMPERATURE	60–75 degrees F
EC	1.0–2.0 mS/cm
PH	5.5–6.5
AIR TEMPERATURE	55–85 degrees F
HUMIDITY	40–80%
LIGHT INTENSITY	150–650 umol/m2/s
DLI	12–21 mol/m2/d
PHOTOPERIOD	12–18 hours/day
CANOPY HEIGHT	4–10 inches
CANOPY WIDTH	3–7 inches
TYPICAL SPACING	2–9 plants/ft2
ROOT SIZE	Small
ROOT ZONE OXYGEN REQUIREMENTS	Low–Medium
GROWING SYSTEMS	Suction Cup Planters, Windowsill Garden, Salad Bowl, Stream of Greens, Bar Cart, Bar Tower, Dinner Table, Picture Frame, Corner Shelf, Coffee Table, End Table, Cabinet Farm, Lettuce Locker, Bathroom Flower Garden, 1020 Tray with Floating Raft

SPINACH

GERMINATION TEMPERATURE	60–70 degrees F
WATER TEMPERATURE	55–70 degrees F
EC	1.0–1.8 mS/cm
PH	5.8–6.2
AIR TEMPERATURE	55–75 degrees F
HUMIDITY	50–75%
LIGHT INTENSITY	150–400 umol/m2/s
DLI	12–21 mol/m2/d
PHOTOPERIOD	10–14 hours/day
CANOPY HEIGHT	3–8 inches
CANOPY WIDTH	3–8 inches
TYPICAL SPACING	2–9 plants/ft2
ROOT SIZE	Small
ROOT ZONE OXYGEN REQUIREMENTS	Medium–High
GROWING SYSTEMS	Stream of Greens, Bar Cart, Bar Tower, Dinner Table, Coffee Table, Cabinet Farm, Lettuce Locker, Bathroom Flower Garden, 1020 Tray with Floating Raft

SOLANACEAE

The *Solanaceae* family includes potatoes, eggplant, tomatoes, and peppers. Most traditional *Solanaceae* crops grow too large for the systems described in this book, but there are an increasing number of breeders developing dwarf tomato and pepper varieties. I highly recommend searching online seed catalogs for dwarf tomatoes and peppers to find varieties that are both interesting and short enough to grow indoors.

DWARF TOMATOES/PEPPERS/EGGPLANTS

GERMINATION TEMPERATURE	70–85 degrees F
WATER TEMPERATURE	65–75 degrees F
EC	1.2–2.5 mS/cm
PH	5.5–6.5
AIR TEMPERATURE	60–85 degrees F
HUMIDITY	40–80%
LIGHT INTENSITY	250–1000 umol/m2/s
DLI	15–30 mol/m2/d
PHOTOPERIOD	12–18
CANOPY HEIGHT	6 inches–40 feet*
CANOPY WIDTH	8–14 inches
TYPICAL SPACING	1–2 plants/ft2
ROOT SIZE	Medium–Large
ROOT ZONE OXYGEN REQUIREMENTS	High

*A commercial greenhouse tomato vine can extend to forty feet or more! The following dwarf varieties recommended shouldn't grow taller than 2 feet when provided adequate light levels. Some varieties will remain under 8 inches tall when provided light levels over 17 mol/m2/d, but they will extend to 18 inches tall when provided 12 mol/m2/d.

DWARF TOMATOES

VARIETY NAME	HEIGHT RANGE	BEGINNER FRIENDLY	NOTES
'Tiny Tim'	8–18 inches		Not as tiny as some of the other dwarf tomato varieties.
'Jochalos'	7–12 inches	Yes	Very short-growing and hardy.
'Yellow Canary'	8–18 inches		
'Pinocchio Orange'	7–12 inches	Yes	One of the best-tasting dwarf tomato varieties. Highly recommended.
'Red Robin'	8–18 inches		Slower and taller-growing than some of the other dwarf varieties.

HERBS—HERBACEOUS

Herbaceous herbs develop no, or very little, woody tissue on their stems. Most herbaceous herbs are fast-growing annuals, unlike woody herbs, which are typically perennials.

CROP	PROPAGATION METHOD	SEEDS PER PLUG	GERMINATION TEMPERATURE (F)	WATER TEMPERATURE (F)	EC (MS/CM)	PH	AIR TEMPERATURE (F)
Basil	Seeds	2–8	65–75	65–80	0.8–2.3	5.5–6.0	70–90
Celery	Seeds	2–5	70–75	60–75	0.8–1.6	5.5–6.5	60–85
Chervil	Seeds	2–6	65–75	60–75	0.8–1.6	5.5–6.5	60–80
Chives	Seeds	4–8	65–70	60–80	1.0–2.2	5.5–6.5	60–85
Cilantro	Seeds	3–5	65–70	60–75	0.7–1.8	5.5–6.5	60–80
Dill	Seeds	3–6	65–70	60–75	0.8–2.0	5.5–6.5	60–80
Fennel	Seeds	3–6	70–85	60–75	0.8–2.0	5.5–6.5	60–80
Lemon Balm	Seeds	3–6	65–70	60–75	1.0–1.6	5.5–6.5	60–75
Mint	Seeds	3–6	65–70	60–75	0.7–2.3	5.5–6.5	60–75
Parsley	Seeds	2–6	65–75	60–75	0.8–1.6	5.5–6.5	60–80
Salad Burnett	Seeds	3–6	60–75	60–75	0.8–2.0	5.5–6.5	60–80
Shiso	Seeds	3–6	65–75	65–75	1.0–1.6	5.5–6.5	60–80
Sorrel, Green	Seeds	2–4	65–70	65–80	0.7–2.3	5.5–6.5	65–85
Sorrel, Red Veined	Seeds	2–8	65–70	60–75	0.7–1.8	5.5–6.5	65–85
Stevia	Seeds or Cuttings	2–5	65–75	65–75	1.0–1.8	5.5–6.5	65–85

WOODY HERBS

Woody herbs include a broad category of plants such as rosemary, lavender, and other herbs with a hard woody stem. Most woody herbs are perennials that prefer drier soil conditions, sometimes making them challenging to grow in a hydroponic garden.

WOODY HERBS	
GERMINATION TEMPERATURE	60–70 degrees F
WATER TEMPERATURE	60–75 degrees F
EC	0.7–2.0 mS/cm
PH	5.5–6.5
AIR TEMPERATURE	60–85 degrees F
HUMIDITY	40–80%
LIGHT INTENSITY	200–650 umol/m2/s
DLI	16–30 mol/m2/d
PHOTOPERIOD	12–20 hours/day
CANOPY HEIGHT	3–16 inches
CANOPY WIDTH	2–12 inches
TYPICAL SPACING	2–5 plants/ft2
ROOT SIZE	Small–Medium
ROOT ZONE OXYGEN REQUIREMENTS	Medium–High
GROWING SYSTEMS	Suction Cup Planters, Windowsill Garden, Stream of Greens, Bar Cart, Bar Tower, Dinner Table, Corner Shelf, Coffee Table, End Table, Cabinet Farm, Lettuce Locker, 1020 Tray with Floating Raft

Genovese basil

LIGHT INTENSITY (UMOL/M2/S)	(DLI (MOL/ M2/D)	PHOTOPERIOD (HOURS/DAYS)	CANOPY HEIGHT	CANOPY WIDTH	PLANTS PER SQ FT	ROOT SIZE	ROOT ZONE OXYGEN REQUIREMENTS	BEGINNER RECOMMENDED
150–650	12–25	12–20	5–16 in	3–8 in	2–5	Medium	Low–Medium	Yes
150–450	12–25	12–20	8–16 in	4–8 in	2–5	Medium	Medium	
150–350	12–21	12–20	6–12 in	4–8 in	2–5	Medium	Medium	
150–450	12–25	12–20	6–10 in	2–4 in	4–9	Small–Medium	Medium	
150–400	12–17	8–16	5–12 in	3–7 in	2–9	Small	Medium	
150–500	12–21	12–20	6–16 in	3–6 in	2–5	Medium	Medium	
150–500	12–21	12–20	6–16 in	3–6 in	2–5	Medium	Medium	
150–350	12–21	12–20	6–10 in	3–5 in	2–5	Medium	Medium	
150–300	12–21	12–20	1–3 in	2–6 in	4–6	Small	Medium	
150–350	12–21	12–20	6–12 in	4–8 in	2–5	Medium	Medium	
150–450	12–21	12–20	5–16 in	4–8 in	2–4	Medium	Medium	Yes
150–450	12–21	12–20	6–12 in	4–12 in	2–4	Medium	Medium	
150–450	12–21	12–20	4–10 in	3–6 in	2–9	Medium–Large	Medium	Yes
150–350	12–21	12–20	3–6 in	2–4 in	4–9	Small–Medium	Medium	
200–450	15–25	12–18	10–16 in	4–8 in	2–5	Small–Medium	Medium–High	

Red vein sorrel grows more slowly and has less flavor than green sorrel but that might be a worthwhile tradeoff for an extra bit of color in your garden.

BABY GREENS/MICROGREENS

GERMINATION TEMPERATURE	70–80 F for most varieties
WATER TEMPERATURE	60–75 F
EC	0.7–2.5 mS/cm
PH	5.5–6.5
AIR TEMPERATURE	60–80 F
HUMIDITY	40–80%
LIGHT INTENSITY	0–350 umol/m2/s
DLI	0–17 mol/m2/d

There is a lot of a variation in the recommended seed density for microgreens for several reasons.

➡ There is the variation in seed size/weight between varieties of the same crop. For example, Grey Striped Sunflower has a much larger seed than Black Oil Sunflower. Using the same grams per square foot for each of these varieties could result in Black Oil Sunflower being planted too densely or Grey Striped Sunflower not dense enough.

➡ The grow out size impacts the optimal seed density. Growing larger plants will require a lower seed density otherwise there will likely be overcrowding.

➡ The size of the tray impacts the optimal seed density. The same grams per square foot will perform differently in large vs small containers due to the ratio of edge space to middle space. It is possible to plant a higher density in a long skinny tray as the plants can extend over the edge of the tray but a large square tray may struggle with overcrowding using that same seeding density.

➡ Climate and airflow impact the likelihood of mold/rot within the microgreen canopy. If the garden has poor airflow it may be difficult to use high seed densities without developing mold in the plant canopy.

Test different seed densities to find out what works best in your unique environment. Growing microgreens is a topic that could fill a book or two of its own. I recommended using microgreen grow guides distributed by seed companies to learn about the many ways to grow microgreens.

CROP	GRAMS PER SQUARE FOOT	LIGHT LEVELS
Amaranth	3–5	50–250
Arugula, Salad	4–7	100–150
Basil	3–5	50–250
Beet	15–20	50–250
Chard	15–25	50–250
Cilantro, Monogerm	13–19	50–250
Corn	100–150	0–20
Kale	7–10	50–250
Kohlrabi	7–12	50–250
Mizuna/Mustard	4–8	50–250
Okra	25–100	0–20
Pea	125–175	50–250
Radish	15–20	50–250
Sunflower	75–175	50–250
Quinoa	0.5–1	50–250

A baby greens blend of Toscano, blue curled and red kale.

EDIBLE FLOWERS

CROP	COMMON/ VARIETY NAMES	PREFERRED EDIBLE PORTIONS	PROPAGATION METHOD	SEEDS PER PLUG	GERMINATION TEMPERATURE (F)	WATER TEMPERATURE (F)	EC (MS/CM)
Acmella oleracea	Toothache Plant, Lemon Drop	Flowers, leaves	Seed	2–5	70–75	65–90	1.0–2.3
Borago officinalis	Borage, Starflower	Flowers, micro-greens	Seed	1–2	60–75	65–75	0.7–1.6
Glebionis coronaria	Chrysanthemum	Flowers, leaves	Seed	2–6	70–80	60–75	0.9–1.8
Lippia dulcis	Dulce Button, Aztec Sweet Herb	Flowers, leaves	Seed	2–5	65–70	65–75	1.0–1.6
Oxalis deppei	Iron Cross	Flowers	Bulb	1		65–75	0.6–2.5
Oxalis hedysaroides	Fire Fern	Flowers, leaves	Cutting	1		65–75	0.6–2.5
Oxalis spiralis subsp. *vulcanicola*	Plum Crazy, Variegated Volcanic Sorrel, Lucky, Zinfandel, Molten Lava	Flowers, leaves	Cutting	1		65–75	0.6–2.5
Oxalis triangularis	False Shamrock, Purple Shamrock	Flowers, leaves, petioles, tubers	Corm	1		65–75	0.6–2.5
Tagetes tenuifolia/ lucida	Marigold, Tangerine Gem, Mexican Mint	Flower, leaves (some varieties)	Seed		75–80	65–85	1.2–2.0
Tropaeolum	Nasturtium	Flowers, leaves	Seed	1–2	60–65	65–75	0.7–2.5
Viola	Pansy, Violet	Flowers	Seed	2–5	60–70	60–75	0.8–1.6

Oxalis spiralis variety 'Plum Crazy'

PH	AIR TEMPERATURE (F)	LIGHT INTENSITY (UMOL/M2/S)	(DLI (MOL/M2/D)	PHOTO-PERIOD HOURS/DAYS	CANOPY HEIGHT	CANOPY WIDTH	PLANTS PER SQ FT	ROOT SIZE	ROOT ZONE OXYGEN REQUIREMENTS	BEGINNER RECOMMENDED
5.5–6.5	70–95	150–600	12–25	12–20	5–12 in	4 in–2 ft	1–3	Large	Low	Yes
5.5–6.5	65–85	200–500	12–21	12–20	1–2 ft	1–2 ft	1–3	Medium	Low–Medium	
5.5–6.5	65–80	150–400	12–21	12–20	6–12 in	4–8 in	2–5	Medium	Medium	Yes
5.5–6.5	65–75	200–350	17–21	12–20	8–16 in	5–18 in	2–9	Small–Medium	Medium–High	
5.5–6.5	60–80	50–450	7–25	8–20	4–8 in	3–7 in	3–9	Small	Medium	Yes
5.5 –6.5	60–80	50–450	7–25	8–20	3–6 in	3–6 in	3–9	Small	Low	Yes
5.5 –6.5	60–80	50–450	7–25	8–20	3–6 in	3–6 in	3–9	Small	Low	Yes
5.5 –6.5	60–80	50–450	7–25	8–20	4–8 in	3–7 in	3–9	Small	Medium	Yes
5.5 –6.5	60–85	150–450	12–25	12–20	6–10 in	4–10 in	2–9	Medium	Medium	
5.5–6.5	65–95	150–600	12–25	12–20	5–10 in	4–24 in	1–3	Large	Low	Yes
5.5–6.5	60–80	150–350	12–21	12–20	4–8 in	4–8 in	2–9	Small	Medium	

Transplanting a Purple Shamrock corm into the Bar Tower garden.

Transplanting a Fire Fern cutting into the Bar Tower garden.

Oxalis triangularis variety 'Purple Shamrock'

ABOUT THE AUTHOR

TYLER BARAS HAS A RANGE OF URBAN AGRICULTURAL EXPERIENCE from homesteading to commercial hydroponics. While completing his B.S. in Horticultural Sciences at the University of Florida, he traveled overseas to study Organic Agriculture in Spain and Protected Agriculture (greenhouse production) in China. After graduation, he worked as a grower for 3 Boys Farm Inc., one of the first certified organic hydroponic farms in the United States. In 2013 Tyler moved to Denver, Colorado, where he worked as the hydroponic farm manager at The GrowHaus. He managed a profitable urban farm while creating a successful hydroponic internship program with a 90 percent job placement rate for graduates. While at The GrowHaus, Tyler started creating educational videos and blog posts about farm tech, which are available on his website FarmerTyler.com.

In 2015 Tyler moved to Dallas, Texas, where he managed the Dallas Grown hydroponic greenhouse and worked as Special Projects Manager for Hort Americas, a commercial hydroponic equipment distributor. While in Dallas, Tyler wrote one of the bestselling hobby hydroponic books, *DIY Hydroponic Gardens: How to Design and Build an Inexpensive System for Growing Plants in Water*. In 2017 Tyler wrote *Roadmap to Growing Leafy Greens and Herbs*, an educational book for new growers and investors interested in commercial hydroponic production of leafy greens in greenhouses and indoor farms. In 2018 Tyler moved to San Francisco, California, where he worked as the New Product Development Senior Grower at the indoor vertical farming company Plenty. In 2020 Tyler relaunched FarmerTyler.com offering horticultural consulting services and educational video content available on *Urban Ag News* YouTube and *Farmer Tyler* YouTube. Tyler's video work has included multiple appearances on P. Allen Smith's *Garden Home*, which airs on the national PBS channel. For more information on Tyler Baras, please visit FarmerTyler.com.

WAYS TO CONNECT WITH FARMER TYLER

www.FarmerTyler.com
www.youtube.com/TheFarmerTyler
www.facebook.com/TheFarmerTyler
www.instagram.com/TheFarmerTyler
www.twitter.com/TheFarmerTyler

ACKNOWLEDGMENTS

Special thanks to everyone who made this book possible!
Angkana Lortpenpien
Colleen Eversman
David & Mary Jo Baras
Hort Americas
Hydrofarm

FARMER TYLER

METRIC CONVERSIONS

Metric Equivalent

Inches (in.)	1/64	1/32	1/25	1/16	1/8	1/4	3/8	2/5	1/2	5/8	3/4	7/8	1	2	3	4	5	6	7	8	9	10	11	12	36	39.4
Feet (ft.)																								1	3	3 1/12
Yards (yd.)																									1	1 1/12
Millimeters (mm)	0.40	0.79	1	1.59	3.18	6.35	9.53	10	12.7	15.9	19.1	22.2	25.4	50.8	76.2	101.6	127	152	178	203	229	254	279	305	914	1,000
Centimeters (cm)							0.95	1	1.27	1.59	1.91	2.22	2.54	5.08	7.62	10.16	12.7	15.2	17.8	20.3	22.9	25.4	27.9	30.5	91.4	100
Meters (m)																								.30	.91	1.00

Converting Measurements

TO CONVERT:	TO:	MULTIPLY BY:
Inches	Millimeters	25.4
Inches	Centimeters	2.54
Feet	Meters	0.305
Yards	Meters	0.914
Miles	Kilometers	1.609
Square inches	Square centimeters	6.45
Square feet	Square meters	0.093
Square yards	Square meters	0.836
Cubic inches	Cubic centimeters	16.4
Cubic feet	Cubic meters	0.0283
Cubic yards	Cubic meters	0.765
Pints (U.S.)	Liters	0.473 (Imp. 0.568)
Quarts (U.S.)	Liters	0.946 (Imp. 1.136)
Gallons (U.S.)	Liters	3.785 (Imp. 4.546)
Ounces	Grams	28.4
Pounds	Kilograms	0.454
Tons	Metric tons	0.907

TO CONVERT:	TO:	MULTIPLY BY:
Millimeters	Inches	0.039
Centimeters	Inches	0.394
Meters	Feet	3.28
Meters	Yards	1.09
Kilometers	Miles	0.621
Square centimeters	Square inches	0.155
Square meters	Square feet	10.8
Square meters	Square yards	1.2
Cubic centimeters	Cubic inches	0.061
Cubic meters	Cubic feet	35.3
Cubic meters	Cubic yards	1.31
Liters	Pints (U.S.)	2.114 (Imp. 1.76)
Liters	Quarts (U.S.)	1.057 (Imp. 0.88)
Liters	Gallons (U.S.)	0.264 (Imp. 0.22)
Grams	Ounces	0.035
Kilograms	Pounds	2.2
Metric tons	Tons	1.1

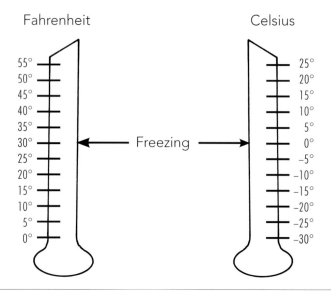

Fahrenheit   Celsius

← Freezing →

Converting Temperatures

Convert degrees Fahrenheit (F) to degrees Celsius (C) by following this simple formula: Subtract 32 from the Fahrenheit temperature reading. Then multiply that number by 5/9. For example, 77°F - 32 = 45. 45 × 5/9 = 25°C.

To convert degrees Celsius to degrees Fahrenheit, multiply the Celsius temperature reading by 9/5, then add 32. For example, 25°C × 9/5 = 45. 45 + 32 = 77°F.

INDEX

T

W